The Irish War of Independence and Civil War

The Irish War of Independence and Civil War

John Gibney (ed.)

PEN & SWORD
HISTORY

AN IMPRINT OF PEN & SWORD BOOKS LTD
YORKSHIRE – PHILADELPHIA

First published in Great Britain in 2020 by
Pen And Sword History
An imprint of
Pen & Sword Books Ltd
Yorkshire – Philadelphia

Produced in association with *History Ireland*: www.historyireland.com

ISBN: 9781526757982

The right of John Gibney to be identified as Editor of this work has been asserted by him in accordance with the Copyright, Designs and Patents Act 1988.

A CIP catalogue record for this book is available from the British Library.

Typeset by Aura Technology and Software Services, India.

Printed and bound in the UK on FSC accredited paper by 4edge Ltd., Hockley, Essex, SS5 4AD.

Pen & Sword Books Ltd incorporates the Imprints of Pen & Sword Books Archaeology, Atlas, Aviation, Battleground, Discovery, Family History, History, Maritime, Military, Naval, Politics, Railways, Select, Transport, True Crime, Fiction, Frontline Books, Leo Cooper, Praetorian Press, Seaforth Publishing, Wharncliffe and White Owl.

For a complete list of Pen & Sword titles please contact

PEN & SWORD BOOKS LIMITED
47 Church Street, Barnsley, South Yorkshire, S70 2AS, England
E-mail: enquiries@pen-and-sword.co.uk
Website: www.pen-and-sword.co.uk

or

PEN AND SWORD BOOKS
1950 Lawrence Rd, Havertown, PA 19083, USA
E-mail: Uspen-and-sword@casematepublishers.com
Website: www.penandswordbooks.com

Contents

Preface

In the aftermath of the First World War, a political revolution took place in what was then the United Kingdom. Such upheavals were common in postwar Europe, as new states came into being and new borders were forged. What made the revolution in the UK distinctive is that it took place within one of the victorious powers, rather than any of their defeated enemies. In the years after the Easter Rising of 1916 in Ireland, a new independence movement had emerged, and in 1918-9 the political party Sinn Féin and its paramilitary partner, the Irish Republican Army (IRA), began a political struggle and an armed uprising against British rule. By 1922 the United Kingdom had lost a very substantial portion of its territory, as the Irish Free State came into being amidst a brutal Civil War. At the same time Ireland was partitioned and a new, unionist government was established in what was now Northern Ireland. These were outcomes that nobody could have predicted before 1914; the essays that follow explore the experience and consequences of the latter phases of the Irish revolution from a wide range of perspectives.

The chapters below have all been drawn from the archives of *History Ireland*, and re-edited; with regards to illustrations, every effort has been made to contact rights holders. If we have missed any, the error will be rectified in any subsequent edition.

Contributors

Jérôme aan de Wiel lectures in history at University College Cork.

John Borgonovo lectures in history at University College Cork.

Tim Carey was formerly administrator of the GAA Museum, Croke Park.

The late Marcus de Búrca was the author of *The GAA: A History*.

Gabriel Doherty lectures in history at University College Cork.

Gavin Foster is Associate Professor in Irish Studies at Concordia University, Montreal.

John Gibney is a historian with the Royal Irish Academy's Documents on Irish Foreign Policy series.

Alexis Guilbride was formerly a research assistant at the Irish Labour History Museum, Dublin.

Barry Keane is a history and geography teacher in Cork.

Bill Kissane lectures in politics at the London School of Economics.

Mary Kotsonouris is a former District Court Judge.

W. J. Lowe is Chancellor and Professor of History at Indiana University Northwest.

Robert Lynch obtained his PhD in history from the University of Stirling, Scotland.

Pearse Lawlor is a retired Northern Ireland civil servant.

Fearghal McGarry is Professor of History at Queen's University Belfast.

Pádraig Óg Ó Ruairc obtained his PhD in history from the University of Limerick.

Mark Phelan obtained his PhD in history from the National University of Ireland Galway.

Pat Poland is the author of *The Old Brigade: The Rebel City's Firefighting Story 1900–1950* (Cork, 2018).

John Reynolds is attached to the Garda Síochána College, Templemore.

Michael Silvestri is Professor of History at Clemson University.

Padraig Yeates was formerly industrial relations correspondent of *The Irish Times*.

Introduction

John Gibney

In the aftermath of the First World War, a political revolution took place in what was then the United Kingdom. Such upheavals were common in postwar Europe, as new states came into being and new borders were forged. What made the revolution in the UK distinctive is that it took place within one of the victorious powers, rather than any of their defeated enemies. In the years after the Easter Rising of 1916 in Ireland, a new independence movement had emerged, and in 1918-9 the political party Sinn Féin and its paramilitary partner, the Irish Republican Army (IRA), began a political struggle and an armed uprising against British rule. By 1922 the United Kingdom had lost a very substantial portion of its territory, as the Irish Free State came into being amidst a brutal Civil War. At the same time Ireland was partitioned and a new, unionist government was established in what was now Northern Ireland.

These were outcomes that nobody could have predicted before 1914, when the prospect of limited devolution within the UK—'Home Rule'—commanded mass support among nationalists, while being opposed by unionists to a degree that threatened civil war. The remarkable rise of Sinn Féin after 1916 was also related to the collapse of the Home Rule cause in the years after the Easter Rising. Originally founded in 1905 as a party advocating economic independence from Britain, Sinn Féin was officially reorganised as a separatist party in October 1917. The most senior of the 1916 survivors, the New York-born maths teacher Éamon de Valera, was installed as its president as the party committed itself to the pursuit of an independent Irish republic. To this end, it promised to lobby for recognition of Irish independence at the peace conference that would follow the war. But the war turned the party into the dominant voice of nationalist Ireland, as it benefited hugely from the wave of popular unease that accompanied the threat to impose conscription on Ireland in 1918.

Sinn Fein took 73 of Ireland's 105 Westminster seats at the first post-war election in December 1918, effectively wiping out the old Home Rule party. The franchise had been expanded and many first time voters, including women over thirty, seemed to cast their lot in with the new party. On 21 January 1919 the new Sinn Féin MPs still at liberty assembled at Dublin's Mansion House under the banner of 'Dáil Éireann' ('assembly of Ireland') and declared Ireland independent. But the same day as the Dáil met, in an unconnected development, two police officers escorting a load of gelignite to a quarry in Soloheadbeg, County Tipperary, were killed in an attack led by Dan Breen and Sean Treacy. The attackers went under the name of the 'Irish Republican Army': the IRA, the name now applied to the older, paramilitary Irish Volunteers (the nationalist militia originally founded in 1913 in support of home rule).

The IRA was quite a localised organisation, fighting the war of the flea in a campaign that became increasingly active from early 1920 onward. The ambushes and assassinations that were the IRA's stock in trade (as advocated in particular by figures like Michael Collins, another 1916 veteran who became one of the principal leaders of the independence movement) posed problems for British forces accustomed to the open warfare of the 'Great War'. British rule in Ireland became more coercive in the years after 1916, a trend which continued as the IRA campaign swung into gear. Trade unions and the labour movement also acted as a third party in the movement for independence (the chapters by aan de Wiel and Guilbride point to the persistence of class tensions throughout the revolutionary period).

Sinn Féin also established a form of guerilla government, in part to fulfil the requirements of their own propaganda but also because they were successfully undermining British rule. As shown by Mary Kotsonouris, they established arbitration courts to defuse local disputes (especially over land) and administer such justice as they could, with the IRA sometimes acting as police. By 1920 Sinn Féin had taken over most of the local authorities in the country and proved remarkably successful at running the machinery of local government themselves. At the same time the IRA also became noticeably more audacious and active. The police and judicial system were targeted and, by the summer of 1920, seemed to be on the brink of collapse. The British compensated for this with draconian legislation and the recruitment of paramilitary forces drawn from demobilised ex-servicemen (such as the Auxiliary Division and 'Black and Tans', examined here by W.J. Lowe). The new forces acquired an unenviable reputation for indiscipline and reprisals against civilians, some of which had official sanction yet virtually all of which were condoned (an issue raised by Borgonovo and Doherty in their essay). Their activities prompted unease among elements of the regular British army along with condemnation in Britain itself.

November 1920 witnessed some of the most notorious incidents of the entire conflict: Bloody Sunday, explored here by Carey and de Burca. On 28 November seventeen Auxiliaries were killed in an IRA ambush led by Tom Barry (a former British serviceman) in Kilmichael in County Cork; parts of Cork City were subsequently burnt down in reprisal attacks, as shown by Pat Poland. Despite this increasing viciousness, from late 1920 the British put out feelers to determine if there was a way out of this intractable conflict.

But before any negotiations could take place with the independence movement, one outstanding issue received a drastic solution.

In 1920 Ireland was partitioned into two jurisdictions, in a move that primarily catered to Ulster unionists rather their co-religionists in the rest of Ireland. In the aftermath of the First World War, the principle of creating new borders was not unique to Ireland. The jurisdiction of the new Belfast parliament—Northern Ireland—extended to six of the nine counties of the historic province of Ulster allowed the maintenance of a Protestant majority in the new parliament. The existence of a substantial Catholic minority was deemed an unavoidable necessity, and, as Pierse Lawlor and Robert Lynch discuss, revolutionary violence took place in and around the new jurisdiction. And once Ulster unionism had been catered for by the new constitutional arrangement, the road was clear to open negotiations with the independence movement in the south. On 11 June 1921 the IRA and the British agreed on a truce, as the Irish War of Independence ended in a stalemate.

The numbers killed were relatively small: 2,100 people between January 1917 and December 1921; to put this in perspective, 20,000 Irish people were killed by the Spanish flu epidemic of 1918-19. But thanks to Sinn Féin's campaign of political resistance and the IRA's guerilla war, the twenty-six counties that became the Irish Free State in December 1922 had been rendered ungovernable from a British point of view, at a time when the British Empire was stretched after the war, and the the resources that the British high command felt would be required to crush the 'rebellion' simply could not be spared (even if their use would be politically feasible).

Following exploratory talks between the Irish independence movement and the coalition government of David Lloyd George in the summer of 1921, in October 1921 negotiations began in earnest and in early December 1921 the Anglo-Irish Treaty was signed, following a dramatic ultimatum from Lloyd George that the alternative was 'immediate and terrible war'. The treaty was far more substantial than the Home Rule on offer in 1912, establishing an 'Irish Free State' as a dominion within the Commonwealth, based on the Canadian model. The fact that this fell short of the fully independent republic sought by Sinn Féin and the IRA caused both organisations to split into pro- and anti-treaty camps, and led directly to the outbreak of a brutal and bloody Civil War six months later. Partition was not, as is commonly thought, the main bone of contention; the key issue was Ireland's constitutional status. The IRA and Sinn Féin had sought a republic; the Free State was nothing of the kind, and the fact that the British monarch would be its head of state proved particularly obnoxious. Michael Collins and Arthur Griffith (the original founder of Sinn Féin) became the leaders of the pro-Treaty faction (both would die in August 1922), while de Valera became the political figurehead for those who opposed the Treaty. Despite attempts at compromise, Civil War broke out in

Dublin in June 1922. The fighting in the capital was over within days. Over the next six weeks the Free State's new army attacked towns held by their opponents, sometimes even landing troops by sea, and soon the Civil War had taken the familiar form of guerilla warfare.

The new government of the Free State, led since August 1922 by W. T. Cosgrave, took the view that they were in a war for their very survival, and as a result went further than the British in terms of the measures they were prepared to stand over. At least seventy-seven republicans were officially executed during the Civil War, some without trials in reprisals for republican attacks; there were also a large number of unofficial reprisal killings by Free State forces. By April 1923 the republican cause was lost, and at the behest of de Valera (who was quite marginal to events during the Civil War), they laid down their weapons in April 1923, thus ending Ireland's 'revolution'.

Naturally, given that the chapters are all drawn from the back catalogue, there are some inevitable gaps, and many of the controversies that have accompanied the study of the period do not feature here. But what these chapters do contain are a range of insights and perspectives into some of the realities of this period of upheaval a century ago, some of the legacies of which still have a resonance today.

Chapter 1

Keeping an eye on the usual suspects: Dublin Castle's 'Personalities Files', 1899–1921

Fearghal McGarry

Beginning in the late nineteenth century, Dublin Castle's 'Personalities Files' span the emergence of Sinn Féin, the Easter Rising and the War of Independence, with the largest number relating to the period 1917–20. As might be expected, the documents provide a rich source of information on leading figures such as Michael Collins and Éamon de Valera—detailing their movements, contacts with other revolutionaries, public speeches, private correspondence and legal struggles with the authorities—but their value is enhanced by the fact that many of the files concern lesser-known political activists, individuals who never became household names but were crucial to the success of the republican movement. Perhaps the most significant aspect is the light that they shed on the security forces and Dublin Castle during these final years of revolutionary violence and administrative chaos.

How was the intelligence in the Personalities Files gathered? For what purpose? What does it tell us about law and order in Ireland and the administration's attempts to contain the growing social unrest and political violence of the period? What do the files reveal about the outlook of the politicians, officials and Crown forces tasked with suppressing the Irish revolution? What do they tell us about the strategies adopted by republicans to overthrow British rule?

The documents, only declassified during the past decade, form a small section of Colonial Office class 904 (better known as 'the Dublin Castle Records'), a series of records of the British administration in Ireland held by the National Archives in London. They originally formed part of the records of the Crimes Special Branch of the Royal Irish Constabulary (RIC), one of two police forces operating in Ireland at this time. The RIC was responsible for law and order throughout the country, while the Dublin Metropolitan Police (DMP) had responsibility for Dublin and the surrounding metropolitan area. It was the latter's G Division (or Special Branch) that would fight the IRA for control of the streets of Dublin during the War of Independence. The Personalities Files were assembled by the RIC, not the DMP, but

1. The documents provide a rich source of information on leading figures such as Michael Collins.

include many documents generated by 'the G' because of Dublin's role as the administrative centre of the republican movement. Given the dearth of surviving material on the DMP, the Personalities Files represent an important source for its crucial G Division.

Like the DMP, the RIC operated a discrete section tasked with monitoring and prosecuting subversives: the Crimes Special Branch (more commonly known as Special Branch). Both special branches shared intelligence but maintained separate staffs and records. Contrary to popular belief, neither was a particularly impressive organisation. Even at the height of the IRA's campaign, 'the G' employed fewer than two dozen men exclusively dedicated to political work, while the RIC's Special Branch consisted not of a nationwide detective force along the lines of Scotland Yard but a confidential records office based in Dublin Castle, staffed by several clerks, a detective inspector and a chief inspector. The vast bulk of intelligence gathered by Special Branch was collected by ordinary RIC men throughout the country, and forwarded to Crimes Special Branch's small office in Dublin Castle. Until the final year of

Dublin Castle's rule, there was no 'secret service' in Ireland; Special Branch did not run undercover agents, rarely recruited informers and made little effort to penetrate the organisations of its enemies. The documents gathered here demonstrate the old-fashioned methods employed by the police: republican premises were kept under observation, train stations and other public places were watched, suspects were shadowed from town to town, and their speeches were recorded by policemen who rarely disguised their identity.

The Personalities Files were generated for a variety of purposes: to gather intelligence on revolutionaries, to compile evidence for their prosecution, to respond to the many inquiries about suspected republican sympathisers that Dublin Castle received, and to justify the dismissal of republicans from public employment. The series documents the correspondence not only of the police but of the offices of the chief secretary, under-secretary, lord lieutenant, government departments such as the General Post Office, and various sections of the Irish and British security forces, including Scotland Yard and MI5. The comments appended to the files by these officials offer revealing insights into the political rationale behind Dublin Castle's decisions and the legal and bureaucratic difficulties they encountered in securing prosecutions.

The largest proportion of files relate to public servants, demonstrating that teachers, clerks, telephonists, excise officers and even postmen were viewed by the regime as potentially dangerous enemies within. The outspoken Borrisoleigh schoolteacher Thomas Bourke was 'a disgrace & a danger to the state', suspected of 'instilling disloyalty into his pupils'. The Strabane postman Cornelius Boyle delivered more than the mail: 'on his travels . . . he is stirring up revolts in the minds of the young men on his walk every day'. Schoolteacher Michael Thornton, a 'devilish ruffian', was dismissed for 'teaching disloyalty and sedition to the children in Furbough School'. Unfortunately for Dublin Castle, teachers, clerks and other public servants belonged to a class particularly drawn to republicanism: young men who were educated, status-conscious and ambitious but frustrated by the lack of social and political opportunities available to them in Ireland under the union. Although some individuals were dismissed on dubious or malicious grounds, the files indicate that the quality of evidence demanded for prosecution, or even dismissal, was generally high: no action was taken in many of these cases despite the RIC's efforts to gather incriminating evidence. Consequently, the Irish administration remained penetrated by republican sympathisers despite its periodic attempts to purge potentially subversive employees.

These sensitive documents, written by officials who would not have expected them to become available for public scrutiny within their own lifetimes, shed much light on the mentality of Britain's officials in Ireland and their response to the growing subversive threat: hostility, anger and frustration are frequently expressed, but so also are incomprehension and some sympathy for individuals tragically caught up in the violence of the Irish revolution. The police reports are particularly illuminating, given that many RIC men felt compelled to report not only on the politics but also on the character and morals of those who fell under their gaze, providing judgements that shed light on the outlook of the official mind and the mores of contemporary society as well as the suspects in question. There was very little, in the early years at least, that escaped the sharp eyes and ears of the local RIC: certainly not a drinking problem, an addiction to gambling, a propensity for keeping bad company or an adulterous affair. Even their social betters did not escape the RIC's perceptive evaluations. Thomas St John Gaffney, a former US diplomat, merited a grudgingly approving assessment as 'a man of wonderful pretensions . . . a man able to live by his wits'.

These frank and often intimately detailed reports provide fascinating insights into the lives of republican activists and the wider community among which they sought to proselytise. The range of propaganda material gathered here is vast: personal letters stopped by the wartime censor, political pamphlets, subversive news-sheets, seditious leaflets, anti-war posters, rebel ballads and even overheard conversations. Republicans active in other countries, particularly the United States, also came under the scrutiny of Special Branch. Most of those who fell under police suspicion were male, but there are files on almost fifty women, including such prominent republicans as Maud Gonne MacBride, Countess Markievicz, Helena Molony and Alice Milligan, as well as lesser-known activists and various victims and opponents of the republican movement.

Most of the files concern republican suspects or victims of republican violence, but a substantial number outline the activities of socialists, trade unionists, feminists, communists and agrarian radicals during a period of disturbed social and economic conditions. For example, Sylvia Pankhurst's visit to Dublin in 1919 to speak to the Irish Women's Franchise League was closely observed. There are also files on deserters, suspect foreign nationals, disgruntled policemen, poison-pen letter-writers, swindlers and paranoid fantasists. There are appeals to Dublin Castle for jobs, money, favours and the redress of grievances, real or imagined. The files also contain letters from several informers and would-be secret agents eager to volunteer their services against the IRA. Kahan Singh Chowdhury, an Indian studying in Dublin in 1920, wrote to the chief secretary offering the use of his 'eastern brain' in the campaign against the IRA. Such men were not always suited to their chosen vocation. P. J. Gartland's request to join the Irish 'secret service' was, bizarrely, supported by the police in his hometown of Liverpool despite his prominent hunchback, drink problem and history of mental instability.

The difficulties faced by the police in securing convictions for political crimes are clearly evident, particularly in troubled areas where local justices and juries were reluctant to convict suspects for political offences and witnesses

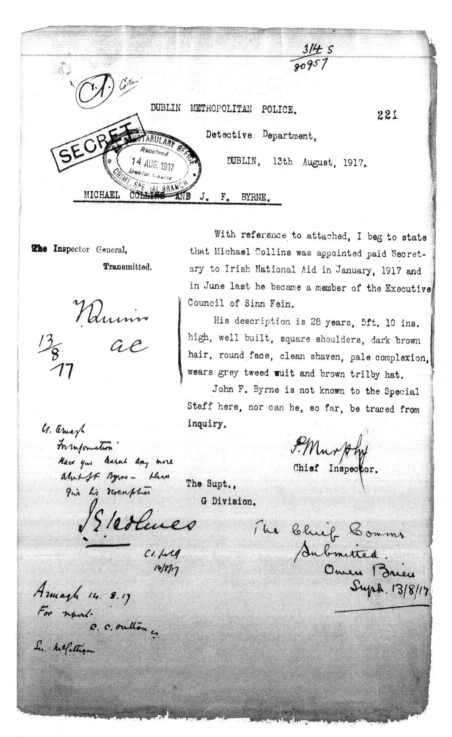

DUBLIN METROPOLITAN POLICE.

Detective Department,

DUBLIN, 13th August, 1917.

221

MICHAEL COLLINS AND J. F. BYRNE.

The Inspector General,

Transmitted.

With reference to attached, I beg to state that Michael Collins was appointed paid Secretary to Irish National Aid in January, 1917 and in June last he became a member of the Executive Council of Sinn Fein.

His description is 28 years, 5ft. 10 ins. high, well built, square shoulders, dark brown hair, round face, clean shaven, pale complexion, wears grey tweed suit and brown trilby hat.

John F. Byrne is not known to the Special Staff here, nor can he, so far, be traced from inquiry.

P. Murphy

Chief Inspector.

The Supt.,
    G Division.

2. An early reference to Michael Collins. (National Archives, Kew)

were invariably unwilling to come forward. The files also demonstrate how republican strategies evolved during the War of Independence. Whereas the rebels of 1916 responded to defeat in an idealistic (or naïve) manner, defiantly admitting their actions and making little effort to evade capture and punishment, the rules had clearly changed by 1919. Republicans found in possession of incriminating documents denied any knowledge of them, publicly repudiating their political sympathies if necessary. Convicted republicans signed undertakings to abstain from political activism to secure early release without any intention of honouring them. Suspects rarely admitted the charges against them—no matter how strong the evidence—and exploited every legal (or illegal) loophole to avoid prosecution or dismissal.

Indeed, it is the increasing inability of the police to respond to the transformed political circumstances that provides the vital context to these files. Before the outbreak of the Great War, the lot of the Irish policeman was not particularly arduous. Although grievances about pay and conditions existed, the police enjoyed a respectable status within their local community. Admittedly, in contrast to the English constabulary, the RIC was an armed force—its 12,000 constables living in military-style barracks outside their home counties for reasons of security and discipline—but it was not generally resented as an alien body, except during periodic outbreaks of political or agrarian tension. The vast majority of RIC men were Catholics—and most, therefore, were nationalists— although the higher ranks of the force, like the judiciary and the upper echelons of the Dublin Castle administration, remained predominantly Protestant and unionist. The force was experienced in dealing with political and agrarian crime and, with its intimate knowledge of the local community, was well placed to chart the volatile political mood of nationalist Ireland. The RIC played a crucial role as 'the eyes and ears of Dublin Castle' and symbolised the power of the British Crown in Ireland. For these reasons, the acceptance of the policeman within his community, and his ability to perform his duties, inevitably came under challenge after 1916.

During the War of Independence, the RIC was placed under intense pressure by the republican movement, which identified the policeman as its principal enemy. The police were ridiculed, intimidated and attacked. Public drilling and the intimidation of witnesses and jurors further humiliated the force by demonstrating its inability to preserve order. The IRA's most effective weapon was the boycott, which began in the summer of 1918. Policemen were shunned by their neighbours, who refused to talk to them, sit beside them at church or conduct business with them. In reality, the police represented more of a soft target than the cutting edge of British imperialism. Many policemen, the inspector general of the RIC reported, opted to resign rather than live 'boycotted, ostracised, forced to commandeer their food, crowded in many instances into cramped quarters

CRANKS & FREAKS OF TO'DAY, FEB. 1901.

IN THE LIGHT
OF
COLD HARD FACTS,
THIS
SELF-CONSTITUTED
AND
WOULD-BE-HEROINE,
NEVER REACHED,
NOR EVEN STARTED
FOR SOUTH AFRICA!
THERE WAS METAL
MORE ATTRACTIVE
IN THE UNITED STATES,
VIZ., FUNDS.
MAUD IS STILL.
PASSING THE HAT
AROUND IN NEW YORK
AT THIS DATE, FEB. 1901.
SHE IS NOT
A BEAUTY
BUT OH! GOSH!!

MAUD GONNE
THE SO-CALLED "IRISH JOAN OF ARC,"
As she appeared in Dublin, equipped to help the
Boers in S. Africa, at the opening of the war in 1899.

3. Cartoon satirising Maud Gonne, from her file. (National Archives, Kew)

without proper light or air, every man's hand against them, in danger of their lives and subjected to the appeals of their parents and their families to induce them to leave'.

Ostracism was followed by assassination. The first meeting of Dáil Éireann in January 1919 coincided with the killing of two policemen at Soloheadbeg, County Tipperary, an attack that shocked many nationalists. By 1920 such murders had become commonplace: some 400 policemen were killed during the conflict. The RIC's strength during times of relative peace—its closeness to the community among whom it lived—became a serious weakness. It was not difficult for determined IRA leaders to cultivate contacts with friendly, frightened or otherwise vulnerable policemen, to intimidate diligent policemen out of their jobs and encourage their less enthusiastic colleagues to remain. A subsequent military report asserted that 'the police service of information had practically broken down by December 1919, owing to the murder of the best and most active members of the RIC and DMP'. By then, the police had also been seriously penetrated. The IRA recruited confidential clerks and Special Branch detectives as informers, while on one famous occasion Michael Collins spent a night locked inside the records room of the DMP.

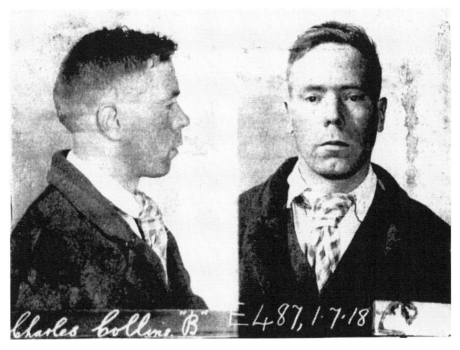

4. Mugshot of Charles Collins, arrested on 19 May 1918 near Brittas, Co. Wicklow, for carrying sixteen sticks of gelignite and other incendiary equipment. (National Archives, Kew)

The streets of Dublin, however, were the front line in the conflict between the police and the IRA. Well known to their putative targets, the G-men who specialised in political work proved particularly vulnerable to IRA attacks. In mid-1919 Michael Collins formed 'the squad' to assassinate these men. The decision was partly pragmatic. Their elimination would remove a vital source of intelligence from the Irish administration, allowing the IRA vital breathing space. But there were also political and symbolic motives. The G-men were the most hated symbols of the British regime, particularly despised for their role in picking out the leaders of the rebellion for execution in 1916. Their killings could be depicted as justifiable, while the British response to them would escalate the conflict. Between July 1919 and May 1920, a dozen DMP men were assassinated. By the end of the IRA's brutal but effective campaign, the DMP's intelligence-gathering capabilities had been destroyed and the force was on the verge of collapse. Remarkably, the DMP was compelled to withdraw from direct involvement in the conflict, its members refusing to carry arms or assume any responsibility for political crime.

The RIC proved more resilient, particularly in terms of morale, but it was placed under enormous strain by the IRA's campaign. The police increasingly came to view entire communities as hostile. By the summer of 1920, even Dublin's Mater Hospital appeared a hotbed of intrigue: 'The community of nuns who manage this hospital, the majority of the medical staff, the nurses and practically all the students are Sinn Féiners or Sinn Féin sympathisers'. These files testify to the RIC's growing inability to meet the republican challenge. Activists could not be located despite continuing to operate within their own areas. IRA men could not be arrested without military support. Although aware of the identity of many of its enemies, the RIC was unable to gather sufficient evidence to prosecute them. Witnesses would not testify against the IRA, and those who were prepared to do so could not be protected. The police's authority in rural areas diminished, increasingly displaced by that of the IRA. By 1920 judges were frequently presented with white gloves, signifying not the peaceful state of the country but the RIC's inability to bring offenders before the courts. Despite misgivings, many RIC men remained loyal to the crown but— increasingly demoralised and anticipating Britain's eventual withdrawal— hundreds resigned, looked the other way or defected to the enemy.

These files illustrate the consequent decline of the police's intelligence capabilities. While many of the earlier files contain detailed and vivid information, the police had clearly lost touch with political crime by 1920. The British Army's 'Record of the Rebellion in Ireland' attributed some of the blame to the RIC's outdated methods and lack of resources:

The Crimes Special Branch depended much more on personal and local knowledge than on organisation and methodical recording . . . The unwise economy which reduced the personnel of the Crimes Special Branch made it almost impossible to keep adequate, up-to-date and reliable records and files. Moreover, nearly every "Crimes Special" report was laboriously written out in longhand and copies were seldom kept. They were passed backward and forward between the central and subordinate officers, thus greatly increasing the opportunities for discovering their contents. The result was that when those men, whose knowledge would have been invaluable during 1920 and 1921, were murdered, the intelligence system in Ireland collapsed for the time being and had to be built up afresh.

Too much responsibility for these shortcomings, however, could be placed on the police, who had little influence over the policies they were expected to execute. Until mid-1920, no coherent security policy was put in place either by the British government or its administration at Dublin Castle, which was regarded by many of the politicians and civil servants who worked within it as dysfunctional and chaotic. The superficially orderly appearance of the Personalities Files masks the confusion that reigned within Dublin Castle. Closer scrutiny provides many examples of these problems. Cooperation and coordination between the army and the police were poor and relations were often strained—as is revealed by such incidents as the forced resignation of the RIC's county inspector for Londonderry, 'who has not the confidence of the military', or the police's anger at the army's failure to come to its assistance following the murder of a sergeant in County Clare. Police advice to Dublin Castle, whose approach oscillated between conciliation and coercion, was frequently ignored: leading republican activists were often released by Dublin Castle despite the RIC's opposition. The resulting tensions between the demoralised police force and Dublin Castle were reflected by the poor relationship between the staunchly unionist lord lieutenant, Field Marshal Lord French, and the inspector general, General Joseph Byrne, until the latter's acrimonious removal from office.

Few of these files concern the final twelve months of the conflict, the period when the British cabinet applied serious effort and resources to the Irish crisis. The appointment of a military officer, Major-General Hugh Tudor, as chief of police signalled a decision to militarise the embattled police force. General Sir Nevil Macready, an officer with a knowledge of both policing and Irish affairs, was appointed general-officer-commanding, Irish command, in March 1920. The RIC was opened to non-Irish recruits, resulting in an influx of demobilised British soldiers (soon known as 'Black and Tans') into the force. These men, and the more effective Auxiliary Division, would earn a notorious reputation for their involvement in reprisals such as the murder of the Sinn Féin lord mayor of Cork, Tomás Mac Curtain (Thomas MacCurtain) and the burning of Cork city. The time-consuming process of gathering evidence for often fruitless civil prosecutions to which many of these files bear testimony was bypassed in favour of an aggressive counter-insurgency campaign relying on martial law, internment and an increasingly dirty undercover war. The RIC's intelligence role was superseded by a reorganised intelligence branch under Brigadier-General Ormonde Winter. These changes placed the IRA under greater pressure but alienated moderate nationalist opinion and shocked international and British opinion, thereby increasing the pressure on both sides for a negotiated end to the conflict. They also spelled the end of the old RIC, many of whose members resented service alongside their less disciplined comrades and the aggressive policies they were now expected to execute.

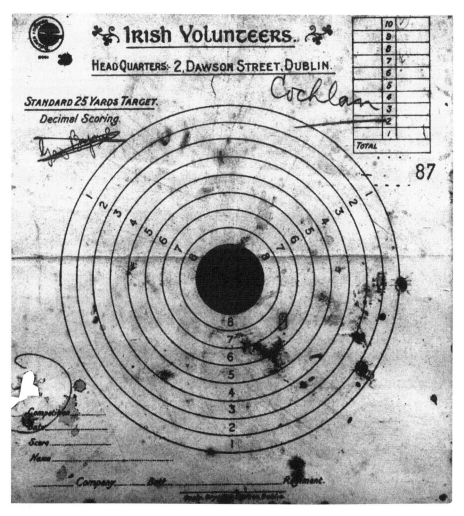

5. Irish Volunteers' target-practice sheet found in 1918 in the Larkfield estate home of Grace Plunkett (née Gifford), wife of the executed Joseph Mary Plunkett. (National Archives, Kew)

The Personalities Files provide a valuable insight into the final years of that force, illuminating diverse aspects of the Irish revolution. For students of the Irish revolution, they represent a rich source of information about the social and political unrest of the last decades of British rule in southern Ireland. The files provide valuable and often vivid insights into the challenges facing the British administration and the background and activities of the young men and women who fought Britain's Crown forces to a stalemate by the summer of 1921.

Chapter 2

Ireland and the Bolshevik Revolution

Jérôme aan de Wiel

In April 1917 the Germans sent Lenin aboard a sealed train from Switzerland to Russia with the aim of starting a revolution and knocking Imperial Russia out of the war. This was part of Imperial Germany's *Revolutionsprogramm*, a strategy conceived to foment trouble in enemy territory. It had failed in Ireland a year before with the defeat of the Easter Rising led by the republican Patrick Pearse and the Irish Volunteers and the Marxist James Connolly and the small Irish Citizen Army. The Rising had not been unanimously welcomed by communist leaders. Karl Radek said that it was a mere 'putsch', while Trotsky warned that the next Irish revolution would have to have the support of the proletariat. Lenin, then living in exile in Zürich, was far more sympathetic, however, and wrote that 'a blow delivered against the British imperialist bourgeoisie in Ireland is a hundred times more significant than a blow of equal weight in Africa or Asia'. In Russia, the October Revolution in 1917 was successful. Lenin spoke of 'the triumphal march of Soviet power'; it was only a matter of time before it spread everywhere.

The Bolshevik leadership decided to pull out of the war to capitalise on the revolutionary *élan*. Adolph Joffe, the leader of the Red delegation, arrived by train in Brest-Litovsk to meet the delegations of the Central Powers. He presented a document containing six points to guarantee a lasting peace. Point three concerned Ireland: 'The possibility to decide freely for national groups within existing states to be attached to other nations or to become independent states.' On 31 December 1917 the US ambassador to Russia cabled Washington on the ongoing negotiations at Brest-Litovsk and included Trotsky's peace programme stipulating that the fate of 'Alsace-Lorraine, Transylvania, Bosnia and Herzegovina, etc., on the one hand, Ireland, Egypt, India, Indo-China etc., on the other [should be] subject to revision'; in other words, *both* the western Allies and the Central Powers should apply the principle of self-determination equally and honestly.

That was before US President Woodrow Wilson presented his 'fourteen points' and his concept of self-determination on 8 January 1918. His secretary of state, Robert Lansing, was not carried away by self-determination and had said to the US's French allies: 'All peoples are not worthy of a republic. One needs

6. Poster for a Dublin Trades Council commemoration of the first anniversary of the October Revolution in November 1918. The establishment of the Bolshevik government in Russia led to expressions of interest and hope in Ireland. (National Library of Ireland, hereafter NLI)

an education to understand what it is.' On 20 January Éamon de Valera, in favour of an Irish republic, reacted very cautiously to Wilson's speech, publicly declaring that it remained to be seen whether he could be trusted. The Sinn Féin president could not have known how right his instincts were.

The establishment of the Bolshevik government in Russia led to expressions of interest and hope in Ireland. The pro-Home Rule *Freeman's Journal* published Trotsky's declaration on self-determination on 4 January 1918. In that same month the rather fractionary Irish Left sent a delegation to meet Soviet plenipotentiary Maxim Litvinov in London. Litvinov assured them that in Russia James Connolly was well known. Some 2,000km away, in Brest-Litovsk, the Germans and Russians eventually signed a treaty on 3 March 1918. The Bolsheviks lost much territory, but Lenin believed that Germany was about to be engulfed by revolution and that it was vital that peace be concluded so that the Central Powers were off Russia's back, which would allow the Bolsheviks to consolidate their revolution and ensure its survival against the counter-revolutionary Whites and other internal enemies.

The Treaty of Brest-Litovsk had dramatic consequences for Ireland. The Germans could transfer their divisions from the eastern to the western front and deliver the knockout blow to the western allies. Their offensive began on 21 March 1918 and at first seemed to be successful. David Lloyd George's cabinet panicked and foolishly extended conscription to Ireland, also including, initially, members of the clergy! This ensured Catholic Church opposition. De Valera secretly liaised with Archbishop William Walsh of Dublin and conscription was defeated thanks to widespread passive resistance. It was the beginning of the end for British rule, as Sinn Féin became the driving force in Irish nationalism. On the western front, the German offensive petered out and defeat was now only a matter of time.

Meanwhile, the western allies sent expeditionary forces to Russia, notably at Murmansk and Arkhangelsk. Lenin said that the country was effectively at war with France and Britain, yet he remained very upbeat. On 7 November 1918, the first anniversary of the Bolshevik revolution, he declared that 'Germany has caught fire and Austria is burning out of control'. He appeared to be right. On 11 November 1918 Germany capitulated, and unrest and dislocation were gripping Germany and Austria-Hungary. Lost Russian territories could be retaken and red flags could be seen in Berlin, Bavaria and Budapest. In December 1918 a political revolution was under way in Ireland, as Sinn Féin overwhelmingly won the general election. It demanded a republic and no partition.

On 21 January 1919 Dáil Éireann met for the first time in Dublin, declared Ireland's independence and announced its intention to send a delegation to the peace conference in Paris. It also issued a 'Message to the Free Nations of the World', reiterating the reality of 'national independence'. The British press largely mocked the event. The same day, at Soloheadbeg, County Tipperary, two policemen were shot dead by Irish republicans, marking the beginning of the War of Independence. De Valera was delighted when left-wingers Tom Johnson and Cathal O'Shannon argued in favour of self-determination in Berne during the Second (Socialist) International in February 1919. In that same month the British *chargé d'affaires* at Arkhangelsk informed London that messages from Moscow had been intercepted, indicating that the Soviets might appoint a representative to this new 'Irish Constituent Assembly' in Dublin. The Foreign Office replied that the Dáil was nothing to worry about.

The Bolshevik leadership might well have been interested in Ireland but had not been impressed by the meeting in Berne. In March the Comintern was founded and Moscow announced its intention to coordinate the worldwide proletarian revolution. Nikolai Bukharin declared 'if we propound the solution of the right of self-determination for the colonies ... we lose nothing by it ... The most outright nationalist movement ... is only water for our mill, since it contributes to the destruction of English imperialism.'

Johnson and O'Shannon were discredited, and the ebullient and full-of-initiative Roddy Connolly, son of James, was now in the ascendant. In April Lenin said that 'the revolution in Hungary gives conclusive proof that in western Europe the Soviet movement is growing and that its victory is not far away'. For European communists or those interested in communist support to achieve self-determination it all sounded very good and promising.

Moscow's voice was encouraging, especially since the Sinn Féin delegation got nowhere near the negotiating table in Paris. Confronted with old-style European diplomacy, Wilson lost much of his idealism but wanted his League of Nations project to see the light at all costs. He was therefore not going to upset the French, and especially the British. The US president did receive an Irish-American delegation but told it firmly that now was not the time to bother him with the everlasting Irish question. It was exactly as Trotsky had predicted: self-determination only concerned territories belonging to the defeated Central Powers. The Germans had been excluded from the peace negotiations and were there only to sign the Treaty of Versailles on 28 June 1919. They refused, however, to support the Irish republicans, their allies of not that long ago, as they knew that the British were more favourably disposed towards their country than the vengeful French. Under no circumstances should London be upset about Irish independence.

The Bolsheviks too had a major problem with self-determination for Ireland: reality. Geography, civil war and economy were going to dictate strategy for Moscow. Berlin and Budapest were two revolutionary hot spots that were out of reach for the Red Army, and the Bolshevik revolutions in those two cities were soon crushed. By the spring of 1920 the Whites were as good as defeated in Russia, but it was at that moment that the army of the recently reborn Poland marched into Ukraine and took Kiev. The Red Army beat the Poles back but

7. Labour leader Tom Johnson—along with William O'Brien he met Russian Commissar of Foreign Trade Leonid Krasin in London, and reported in January 1921 to a meeting of Labour officials and Dáil ministers that the Russians had become far more moderate in their support for an Irish republic. (NLI)

was decisively beaten by Józef Piłsudski during the Battle for Warsaw in August 1920. On paper, the Red Army looked formidable with its 4.6 million men, but in fact it was poorly trained and equipped. If Berlin and Budapest were out of reach and Poland could not be beaten, it was not even worth mentioning Dublin or Cork. Stalin wrote in *Pravda* that the Polish offensive had been orchestrated by the Entente powers (France and Britain).

Meanwhile, in London Lloyd George was opposed to any direct intervention in Russia, as it was too expensive. After the war the British needed to put their financial house in order. In November 1919 the prime minister had spoken of normalising relations with Bolshevik Russia. In the spring of 1920 the British began talks with the Russians to restore trade. The Bolsheviks were most definitely interested, as their country's economy needed to recover before any large-scale foreign projects could be undertaken. On 16 March 1921 the Anglo-Russian Trade Agreement was signed by Commissar of Foreign Trade Leonid Krasin. The British ended their blockade of Russia and both sides agreed to cease hostile propaganda campaigns.

The trade negotiations had repercussions for Moscow's commitment to self-determination for Ireland. Labour leaders William O'Brien and Tom Johnson met Krasin in London and reported in January 1921 to a meeting of Labour officials and Dáil ministers that the Russians had become far more moderate in their support for an Irish republic. Ireland's condition was not favourable for a Bolshevik revolution, and that was all that Moscow was interested in. Several 'soviets' sprang up in Ireland and the red flag flew in many places, but these were isolated incidents whose importance should not be overestimated. The farmers had got much land back thanks to Land Acts introduced before the First World War. State property or collectivisation would have been immediately rejected. Newspapers regularly reported on red terror in Russia and the regime's war on religion. The Catholic Church warned against Bolshevik atheism. British intelligence conducted a campaign depicting Irish republicans as closely associated with the Bolsheviks.

De Valera knew that he had to remain cautious and remembered the power displayed by the Church during the conscription crisis. What if that power was suddenly directed against republicans? Despite Woodrow Wilson's lack of enthusiasm for Ireland in Paris, de Valera set off to the USA, where he stayed from June 1919 until December 1920. His mission was to secure official recognition for the Irish Republic, to get support from the American people and to get money for the cause. The Wilson government never recognised the Irish Republic, however, and de Valera was soon at loggerheads with Irish-American republican groups and personalities, who had no desire to be bossed around by him.

Yet Dr Patrick McCartan, the Dáil's envoy to the USA, had established contacts with Ludwig Martens, the Russian representative. In 1920 he negotiated

a draft treaty with the Russians that stipulated the mutual recognition between the two revolutionary governments, the establishment of commercial relations and even the entrusting 'to the accredited representative of the Republic of Ireland in Russia the interests of the Roman Catholic Church'. The last point was obviously meant to neutralise a possible Irish ecclesiastical backlash and was rather naïve. When shown the draft treaty, de Valera was not particularly enthused but told McCartan to send it to the cabinet in Dublin. He also wanted an Irish delegation to go to Moscow. The cabinet agreed, but only if nothing could be expected from the US government. Caution remained. In June 1920, however, the Dáil decided that a delegation should be sent with the aim of establishing diplomatic relations; the issue of the draft treaty was not broached. It was by now clear that de Valera's American recognition tour was less successful than anticipated.

The Dáil's decision was not unanimously approved. Sinn Féin diplomats George Gavan Duffy and Seán T. Ó Ceallaigh reported from Paris that Ireland's emerging links with Bolshevik Russia were counterproductive and would further isolate Ireland on the Continent. Nonetheless, de Valera was now anxious that McCartan proceed to Russia but refused to grant him plenary powers. McCartan said that if a treaty was concluded he would ask the Russians to ship over 50,000 rifles. He eventually arrived in Russia on 6 February 1921. There he was sent on a political wild-goose chase. After several days of waiting, he first met Maxim Litvinov, who was, in the end, honest enough to tell him that 'on account of conditions both inside and outside Russia it would be inadvisable for the Russian government to do anything for Ireland'. Litvinov also mentioned the importance of the current trade negotiations with the British.

9. Roddy Connolly in 1976. In the summer of 1921 he was in Moscow for the Third Comintern Congress. (RTÉ Stills Library)

McCartan then travelled to Moscow to meet Commissar for Foreign Affairs Georgy Chicherin. Again, he was made to wait several days before being granted a not particularly productive meeting. Chicherin said that the Irish republicans were 'not in military control' and even asked whether 'if Russia gave [Ireland] recognition would the Irish people not expect more assistance than [Russia] could give [her]'? Of course, this was true after the Battle for Warsaw, but Chicherin was only looking for excuses to get rid of McCartan. According to McCartan, Chicherin was mainly interested in the Irish Citizen Army, not so much the republicans; he even said, correctly, that '[we] have been informed that [you] are hostile to communism' and was convinced that the republican movement in Ireland 'was inspired by American dollars'. Dollars had indeed been pretty much on de Valera's mind when he embarked for the US. Finally, Chicherin came perhaps to the crux of the matter when he declared that 'they could not assist [Irish republicans] with such things as rifles and ammunition'. McCartan would take the train and boat back home.

As for Roddy Connolly, he was in Moscow for the Third Comintern Congress in the summer of 1921, during which little was said on colonial issues and far more on the failure of revolution in Europe. He met Lenin and gave him a report entitled 'The conditions of Ireland, 1 July 1921', outlining the latest actions of the IRA and his unrealistic belief that the population could embrace communism provided that 'considerable extraneous assistance' was provided— in other words, Russian assistance. He also felt that the republican leadership would eventually agree with the British on dominion status for Ireland. He was right on the last point. On 6 December 1921 Arthur Griffith and Michael Collins signed the Anglo-Irish Treaty. A few months later the Civil War began, as the treaty fell far short of what de Valera and his followers wanted: a republic for the whole island. In London in February 1922 Leonid Krasin told Irish visitors that his government was willing to have 'close political and commercial relations' with the newly formed Irish Free State.

In July 1922, still in London, Connolly told Mikhail Borodin of the Comintern that the IRA would be able to wage guerrilla warfare, obliging the British army to intervene and resulting in the destruction of the Free State. Borodin did not mince his words: 'It is my firm opinion that they will crush the republicans … It is really laughable to fight the Free State on a sentimental plea. They want a republic. What the hell do they want a republic for?' Borodin was right in his prediction, but showed that idealism for small nationalities was only of interest to the Bolshevik leadership if it suited its interests at the right moment. In the end, early Irish–Soviet relations were *realpolitik* all round. It was only in the mid-1970s that both countries established official diplomatic relations.

Chapter 3

'Oh God, what did I do to deserve this?' The life and death of Detective Sergeant John Barton

Padraig Yeates

If he died today in the line of duty Detective Sergeant John Barton of the Dublin Metropolitan Police would probably be declared a national hero. The *Irish Times* editorial of 1 December 1919 proclaimed him 'one of the bravest, most vigilant, and most intelligent defenders' of the city's peace. The *Irish Independent* said that 'Sergeant Barton seemed possessed of an instinct for tracking down criminals and his name alone was sufficient to inspire terror in the hearts of evil doers'.

Obviously it was not sufficient to deter the IRA's director of intelligence Michael Collins, although he designated no less than three groups of Volunteers to carry out the task. On 29 November 1919, all three converged on Barton when he was only yards from the safety of the new Central Police Station on Great Brunswick (now Pearse) Street. The fatal shot was probably fired by Seán Treacy, who had led the Soloheadbeg ambush in which RIC Constables James McDonnell and Patrick O'Connell were killed, sparking the War of Independence the previous January. Barton was hit at such close range that there were scorch-marks on his clothes.

He managed to draw his revolver and fire one round before exclaiming, 'Oh God, what did I do to deserve this?' and collapsing on the ground. The question still preyed on his mind as a Dublin Fire Brigade ambulance took him to Mercer's Hospital. He said to the crew, 'They have done for me. God forgive me. What did I do?'

John Barton was born in April 1880 into a farming background at Firies, County Kerry. He joined the Dublin Metropolitan Police in February 1903, and at six feet four and a quarter inches he certainly met the DMP criteria of being physically impressive, although he walked with a slight stoop. Barton was one of the best-known members of B Division, which was based in the south-east quadrant of the inner city. He only transferred to the detective or G Division of the DMP on 10 October 1919, less than seven weeks before he was killed. He was the fourth DMP member, and third G Division detective, to be killed in the War of Independence.

He was, however, well known and feared in labour as well as republican circles long before that. As Irish Citizen Army (ICA) veteran Frank Robbins

10. Sergeant John Barton (second from the left) in Dublin Castle on 2 February 1917 after he had been awarded his first King's Police Medal (third medal on the right) for his services in the Easter Rising, when he disregarded orders to remain in barracks. He was awarded a second in early 1918 for his services in 1917, the only member of the DMP to win two. (Garda Stephen Moore)

said, 'He did more than his duty'. Barton arrested over forty people during the 1913 Lockout and helped apprehend a dozen workers involved in a Christmas Day fracas on City Quay when DMP Sergeant James Kiernan was thrown in the Liffey. One member of the Irish Transport and General Workers Union (ITGWU), Patrick Higgins, tracked down by Barton, was subsequently sentenced to ten years for his role in the affair. Such activities were not designed to make a policeman popular. Nor was his apprehension earlier that month of a 'chocolate gang'. John Kearney, aged eleven, was sentenced to a month in Summerhill, and Michael Donegan, aged twelve, to five years in Glencree for larceny of chocolate. John Kelly, aged thirteen, and Joseph Grimes, aged eleven, were put on £5 bail and eighteen months' probation each.

It was in 1916 that Barton gained real notoriety. He ignored orders to remain in barracks during the Easter Rising. Undeterred by the fatal shootings of three colleagues and the wounding of seven others, he prowled the streets apprehending rebels and looters. After the surrender he went to Richmond Barracks to assist G Division detectives in identifying leading rebels. Presumably he was working as a 'buckshee' detective on his own time in the hope of a transfer to the detective division. Seán Murphy of the Irish Republican Brotherhood (IRB) later testified that it was Barton who picked out Seán MacDiarmada, saying, 'Sorry, Seán, but you can't get away that easy. There will be six for you in the morning, I think'—a passing reference to the number of soldiers who made up a firing squad.

Frank Robbins recalled Barton stopping in front of Joseph Connolly to tell him that his brother Seán had been killed in the Rising. When Joseph replied, 'He died for his country', Barton retorted that 'He was a disgrace to his country'. When he saw Michael Donnelly, another ICA member and an ITGWU activist, Barton, in a reference to the Lockout, asked, 'Do you remember the day you laughed at me going down the quays?' Donnelly answered, 'Hasn't the cat leave to laugh at the king?' Barton growled 'I suppose so', and passed on. Robbins later accused Barton of badgering one vulnerable ICA prisoner so much that the man attempted suicide.

Other detectives participated in the identification process that day but it was Daniel Hoey and John Barton who left the most lasting impression. Over thirty years later Robert Holland, a member of the republican youth organisation Na Fianna Éireann, remembered the pair 'as they cynically walked slowly down along the hall with a sneer on their faces'. Barton used a walking stick to identify important figures to the military, Hoey an umbrella.

Nor did these activities distract Barton from his normal police duties. A major anomaly of the Rising is that, although the bulk of the looting in Easter Week occurred north of the River Liffey, most of those arrested for illegal possession of goods lived south of the river. Of the 425 people convicted of this offence in the weeks after the Rising, 296 were arrested by John Barton, or Constable 37B, as he is listed in the DMP Prisoners Books. This included most of the women arrested. They comprised fifty-eight per cent of all those sentenced in the police magistrates' courts in May 1916 and twenty-seven per cent of those convicted in June. Barton had single-handedly transformed the criminal profile of Dublin from one in which men always constituted the vast majority of culprits to one in which they were supplanted by women, albeit only for a few weeks.

He returned to the fray on 18 June, when the first public demonstration took place in support of the rebels. It began when a group of 400 'girls' carrying a 'republican flag' gathered outside Christ Church Cathedral following requiem masses at the Church of the Immaculate Conception on Merchant's Quay for Tom Clarke and at St Mary of the Angels on Church Street for Eamonn Ceannt. Both churches were in the charge of the Franciscans, the most sympathetic religious order in the city to the republican cause.

The 'girls' accumulated a crowd of 2,000 people as they advanced down Dame Street towards O'Connell Street. They booed the British sentries outside Dublin Castle and the Bank of Ireland in College Green before being intercepted by the DMP outside the Ballast Office. The police were determined to prevent

11. Rebel prisoners under guard in Richmond Barracks, May 1916. Barton
    played a leading role in identifying the leaders. (NLI)

them from crossing the river. Trouble erupted when the police attempted to
seize the flag. Tram destination boards and collection boxes for the Volunteers'
Dependants' Fund (one of a number of charities set up to help the families of
republican prisoners) were among the missiles used to counter police batons.
Seven young men and three women were arrested and charged with 'Doing
an act likely to prejudice the Defence of the Realm; Assaulting the Police etc.'
Although the chief police magistrate, E. G. Swifte, decided to deal with the cases
under the Public Order Acts rather than employ the more draconian penalties
contained in the Defence of the Realm Act, the accused were unapologetic. Two
of the men, Percy Forrester and John Halpin, freely admitted striking policemen
but became indignant at the suggestion that they kicked any. Catherine Bolger
admitted not only kicking a policeman but also hitting another in the face and
calling them all 'Saxon curs and Saxon dogs'. At least two of the defendants,
sixteen-year-old Denis Fitzpatrick and twenty-two-year-old Christina Caffrey,
had taken part in the Rising but had evaded arrest. Fitzpatrick was let off with
a caution and Caffrey was fined forty shillings.

   The fact that Fitzpatrick and Caffrey were apparently 'unknown to the
police' underscores the woefully inadequate state of DMP intelligence and
suggests that the G Division was not as omniscient as it is sometimes portrayed.
In fact, only a minority of members were involved in the detection of political
as opposed to ordinary crime. Curiously, the two policemen most badly injured
in the fracas outside the Ballast Office were Constables Barton and Henry
Kells. Kells would soon be acting as another 'buckshee detective' in the hope
of promotion to G Division. Unlike Barton, he did not achieve his ambition.

In fact, he did not long outlive Barton, being shot dead on 24 April 1920 at the junction of Camden Street and Pleasant Street while operating in plain clothes. His last words, if any, are unrecorded.

On 2 February 1917 Barton was awarded the King's Police Medal (KPM) 'for conspicuous gallantry and exceptional ability and devotion to duty during the past year'. This was the highest award a police officer could receive. According to the statement issued to the newspapers, it was in recognition of Barton's being

> Instrumental in the detection and apprehension of a very large number of criminals. During the first night of the rebellion he arrested at great personal risk twenty-seven persons who were looting in the vicinity of O'Connell Bridge, which was dominated by rebel fire, and on the same night, with the assistance of another officer, he arrested two armed men who were carrying a large quantity of ammunition.

He was promoted to sergeant on the same day, which saw his pay rise from £1 14s 8d a week to £2 0s 8d, and it would rise again to £2 12s 8d on his transfer to G Division on 10 October 1919. These very substantial increases totalled over fifty per cent, but they hardly explain his dedication to duty at a time when many members of the DMP were engaged in a retreat from the increasingly hostile streets. Between 1913 and 1919 the number of arrests carried out by the DMP fell from 11,065 to 4,394, summonses served fell from 28,334 to 16,261 and assaults on constables fell from 338 to 51. Some G Division detectives, such as Eamon Broy and David Neligan, became double agents for Collins, as did members of the uniform branch such as Joe Kavanagh and Maurice Aherne.

12. DMP Commissioner Lt Col. Sir Walter Edgeworth Johnstone (with stick) and Assistant Commissioner Denis Barrett (to his right) with thirty-nine members of the G Division, shortly after they were disbanded on 1 February 1922. Four of the eleven DMP members killed in the War of Independence were G Division detectives. Contrary to popular belief, most were ordinary detectives and unwilling recruits to political work. (Superintendent Brendan Connolly)

In fact, much of the information leading to the assassination of G Division members came from their fellow officers. Far from following their example, Barton received a bar to his KPM in 1918 in recognition of his continuing exemplary conduct, including the dramatic arrest of an armed Boer officer for desertion in 1917. He was the only member of the DMP to receive two KPMs.

Barton remained an aberration, accumulating enemies as he went. Michael Noyk, who was a leading defence lawyer for republicans in the British courts, recalled that his very first case was representing a man accused by Barton of larceny of a military service rifle. When Noyk met Barton in the Empire Music Hall on Dame Street later he twitted him about losing the case, asking, 'Did you ever get the gun?' Barton snapped, 'I think you know more about it than I do'. A newly recruited teenager to Collins's intelligence operation, Charlie Dalton, who was to have a somewhat chequered career of his own, said that Barton

> Was held in the highest esteem by the publicans, pawnbrokers and other commercial men, due to the fact that he had established a unique method in the tracing of petty larceny and illegal pawning of stolen goods. In carrying out his routine police duties, he had many newsvendors and minor thieves of the pick-pocket variety in his power, and he utilised this type of informer for checking on the movements of prominent wanted volunteers.

Frank Henderson, who was a 1916 veteran and commandant of the 2nd Battalion in Dublin, described 'the well-known Johnny Barton' as 'an efficient criminal detective … who had only undertaken "political work" after the Republican Government had begun to exact the death penalty on enemy intelligence personnel. Barton was warned when he commenced his spying but did not heed the notices sent to him.'

Why Barton pursued a career path that meant almost certain death will probably never be known. A single man with no obvious interests outside the job, he was single-minded in pursuit of the enemy, oblivious to the rapidly changing political climate.

When nineteen-year-old Vinnie Byrne was asked by Mick McDonnell, the head of Collins's newly organised 'squad' within the Dublin IRA, 'Would you shoot a man, Byrne?', the young carpenter replied, 'It's all according who he was'. When McDonnell said, 'What about Johnny Barton?', Byrne said, 'Oh, I wouldn't mind'. Barton had earlier raided Byrne's home. After finishing work that day, he was one of the gunmen who cornered Barton at 6 pm on College Street and left him to die wondering what he had done to deserve such a fate. To some he was a hero; to others, such as Fianna boy Robert Holland who remembered him from Richmond Barracks, Barton was 'the very scum that kept us in British bondage'.

Chapter 4

Smoking gun? British government policy and RIC reprisals, summer 1920

John Borgonovo and Gabriel Doherty

O n 17 April 1920, a coroner's jury investigating the shooting of Cork lord mayor (and IRA brigade commander) Tomás MacCurtain issued its famous finding of 'wilful murder' against Prime Minister David Lloyd George and top civil and police officials in Ireland. The verdict provoked a predictable response from, amongst others, the *Irish Times*, which mocked it

Date Unknown, Location Unknown, Unknown Persons

13. RIC constables c. 1920. The Prescott-Decie letter suggests the involvement in murderous reprisals of such regular, Irish-born members of the RIC and not just their Black and Tans and Auxiliary counterparts, and the commencement of reprisals months earlier than commonly believed. (Garda Archives)

as 'a novel stroke of Celtic fantasy' that certain Irish people would accept only because they were 'blinded by political passion and prejudice' and willing to attribute to the RIC 'the spirit of revenge which would dominate their own furious minds if they walked in hourly peril of the assassin's pistol'.

One wonders, however, whether the leader-writer would have been quite so dismissive had he been privy to a letter written only a few weeks later by one of the most senior officers of the RIC and addressed to one of the most influential civil servants in Dublin Castle, which frankly debated the merits of a 'new policy' of official 'secret murder' of the regime's opponents. The letter reveals a disturbing policy of assassination sanctioned by the highest level of the British government in Ireland. As such, we believe, it must lead to a fundamental reappraisal of the approach adopted by that government in this, one of the most sensitive aspects of the entire Irish War of Independence.

The traditional view of 1919–21 attributes British reprisals in Ireland to drink-fuelled and war-traumatised Black and Tans or Auxiliaries, who, outraged by cowardly assaults on their comrades, wreaked their vengeance on local civilians and were facilitated by superiors who looked the other way. According to this assessment, the growing incidence of 'unauthorised' reprisals in the autumn and early winter of 1920–1 forced the government to officially sanction the policy in December 1920, only to abandon it the following June in the face of mounting public criticism. By contrast, while attention has been paid to police attacks on property, there has been far less focus on the assassinations of republican activists that frequently accompanied RIC arson reprisals.

Some historians have noted disturbing testimony from high-ranking government officials that indicated explicit encouragement of such a policy. Dublin Castle senior civil servant Mark Sturgis reported that his superior, Under-Secretary Andy Cope, preferred the assassination of IRA gunmen to arson, as 'to shoot a known bad man . . . is morally much more defensible than this stupid blind work'. On a different occasion Sturgis quoted Cope as saying that 'The RIC are not out of hand but are systematically led to reprise by their officers'. A senior British civil servant claimed that Prime Minister David Lloyd George 'strongly defended the murder reprisals'. Furthermore, Field Marshal Sir Henry Wilson attended a meeting with Winston Churchill and a member of the staff of Major-General Hugh Tudor (of whom more anon), during which planned police assassinations of targeted Irish republicans were discussed, with Churchill remarking that on this matter Tudor 'could rely on LG [Lloyd George] to back him'. Most damagingly, in early July 1920 Sir Henry Wilson recorded that Lloyd George not only believed that such an assassination policy existed (a belief that Wilson described as 'ridiculous') but that 'he was gloating over this and hugging it to his heart as a remedy for the disgraceful state of Ireland'.

MUNSTER No. 1 DIVISION

Divisional Commissioner's Office.

Limerick. 1st June 1920.

To The Assistant Under Secretary

I beg to report that the state of this Division
is steadily getting worse . The efforts of the Sinn Feiners
are principally directed to getting rid of the Police,so
that the Laws of Kingdom may become wholly inoperative.
For the same reason they are endeavouring to reduce all
Courts of Justice , and Inquests to a farce. In lieu of
British Courts , they are establishing their own. County
Kilkenny at present seems a favourite spot for these courts.
Probably because it is so weakly garrisoned with Police
and Military. The Sinn Fein method of maintaining their
hold is very simple, they threaten all who oppose them
and if that is not sufficient murder them. The Loyal
people and the Law abiding people who are considerable in
number are completely terrorised. The openly say
" What is the good of being Loyal to the British Government
which let us down every time "., A fine old man said to
me yesterday " my three sons were killed in the War ,my
only daughter died of disease while nursing, and now I am
being robbed of my land ,and yet I am loyal ? God knows why"

The situation with the police themselves has
been very ticklish. They have been very near throwing up
the sponge . They consider they have been let down by the
Government and that they have been unsupported. Their arguments are hard to find answers to . Let no one suppose
they are frightened - they are not. I dont wish to blow
my own trumpet but merely to show how close a shave it
has been , in saying they have been held together by the
influence of myself,and the Officers of the R.I.C. Major
General Tudor's visit was of great value. We can hold
them now for a time but if the support promised was to
fail , the situation would be, I fear, beyond retrieving.
I have been told the new policy and plan and I am satisfied,
though I doubt its ultimate success in the main particular-
the stamping out of terrorism by secret murder. I still
am of opinion that instant retaliation is the only course
for this , and until it is stamped for good and all, the
same situation is likely to recur. The I.R.A. are
improving their Organisation .- I expect more frequent and
better prepared attacks on Barracks.

I trust that now any demands of mine will be
more promptly met. It is unnecessary I think to say
more at this moment. When the support we are promised
arrives , we shall know how to employ it in carrying out
the policy outlined to me. Meanwhile we hang on.

C. Prescott Decie

Brig. Genl.

14. The Prescott-Decie letter of 1 June 1920 can be found in Crime Special
Branch Other Papers, Box 24, National Archives of Ireland. No related
material accompanies the one-page document, which appears to have
become separated from a larger administrative file and left behind during
the evacuation of Dublin Castle in 1922. (NAI)

Up to now no evidence has been found that directly links assassination reprisals to Dublin Castle. The letter in question, however, provides just such a link in the chain of authorisation so memorably condemned by the MacCurtain jury. The letter, of 1 June 1920, from Brigadier-General Cecil Prescott-Decie, then a divisional commissioner of the RIC, to John Taylor, the former assistant under-secretary in Dublin Castle (a noted hawk on security matters who had consistently opposed concessions to nationalist opinion), challenges many of the assumptions concerning British policy in Ireland during 1920–1. It suggests the involvement in murderous reprisals of regular, Irish-born members of the RIC and not just their Black and Tan counterparts, and the commencement of reprisals months earlier than commonly believed. Indeed, the proactive rather than reactive nature of the policy and its explicit 'top-down' sanction by top officials in the 'Irish government' bring into question whether the word—nay, the very concept of—'reprisal' needs to be fundamentally revised.

The Prescott-Decie memo must be placed within the context of developments in the critical spring of 1920. In the year's first months, Sinn Féin assumed control of elected municipal bodies across the country and created Dáil courts that stymied the British judicial system in Ireland. Simultaneously, IRA units launched an offensive against police patrols and posts, resulting in the systematic abandonment and destruction of vulnerable RIC barracks around the country. Further isolated by a social and economic boycott of the RIC and their families, police morale threatened to collapse. By May some rank-and-file constables were lobbying for military and civil reinforcements, while others advocated disarming the force entirely. Only a week before Prescott-Decie's letter, RIC Inspector-General Smith reported the resignation and retirement of 250 constables during April alone, and openly confessed that if the present conditions continued the men under his command would run amok *en masse*.

Facing a rapidly deteriorating security situation, the British administration reorganised and recalibrated its approach to the new parameters of the Irish question. On the political front, the Government of Ireland Act began its almost year-long passage through Westminster. Administratively, March through May saw significant personnel changes in the upper echelons of the British political, military and police establishments in Ireland. New personnel arrived in Dublin Castle as John Anderson was appointed under-secretary and Sir Hamar Greenwood replaced Ian Macpherson as chief secretary. Within the security forces, Sir Neville Macready assumed the role of commander-in-chief of the British Army in Ireland, while T. J. Smith took over the position of inspector-general of the RIC and Major-General Hugh Tudor was appointed as the government's adviser on policing matters. The Irish police became an even more militarised body, as constables received heavier weapons and equipment, and began to be reinforced by newly hired British military veterans enrolled into the force—soon known as the 'Black and Tans'. During the same

15. RIC constables drilling with fixed bayonets c. 1920. By late spring 1920 the RIC became an even more militarised body, with heavier weapons and equipment. (Garda Archives)

period, the RIC was reorganised into divisional areas, and high-ranking British Army officers were appointed to many of the commissioner posts, including the highly decorated Lieutenant-Colonel Gerald Smith and Brigadier-General Cecil Prescott-Decie.

Prescott-Decie was a career officer with significant experience in various colonial conflicts in Africa before serving as a divisional artillery commander on the Western Front during the First World War. Appointed divisional commissioner for the Munster No. 1 area, with responsibility for three counties in North Munster, he took up his post in Limerick city, which was then a hotspot of republican activity. Amongst his military counterparts he had a reputation for a cavalier attitude towards the legal use of lethal force, being memorably condemned by General Macready for believing 'that martial law means that he can kill anybody he sees walking along the road whose appearance may be distasteful to him'. As will be seen, however, even Prescott-Decie baulked at what was to be asked of him by the government (albeit on grounds of efficacy rather than morality).

Awake to the desperate state of the police in his area, Prescott-Decie wrote to Assistant Under-Secretary John Taylor on 1 June 1920. Amid a surging republican campaign, the brigadier reported the collapse of the British judiciary and desperation within the loyalist population. It was the sinking morale of his constables that worried him most, however. 'The situation with the police themselves has been very ticklish,' he wrote. 'They have been very near throwing up the sponge.' His men had been buoyed by a recent visit by General Tudor, but unless promised assistance arrived 'the situation would be, I fear, beyond retrieving'. It was here that he made remarks that only make sense in the context of revised official government policy, as outlined by Tudor during his recent tour: 'I have been told the new policy and plan and I am satisfied, though I doubt its ultimate success in the main particular—*the stamping out of terrorism by secret murder*. I still am of opinion that *instant retaliation* is the only course for this, and until it is stamped for good and all, the same situation is only likely to recur.'

On its own, the imperfect syntax of the first sentence renders its meaning uncertain; in isolation, it could be construed as suggesting that 'secret murder' was the defining feature of 'terrorism' rather than the 'new policy' of the British government. But the second sentence—which counterpoints Prescott-Decie's preferred line of action ('instant retaliation') to that endorsed by government—makes it clear that the 'secret murder' referred to was to be carried out by the RIC.

Here is indisputable evidence that Dublin Castle authorised an assassination campaign against its republican opponents. Though Black and Tan and Auxiliary cadets often perpetrated these killings (and the more frequent attempted killings), this statement pre-dates their substantial deployment in Ireland. Far from striking out of ill-disciplined rage, it would appear that the constabulary were simply implementing the cold-blooded direct orders of their superiors. While both republicans and British officials subsequently found it politically convenient to blame these assassinations on 'foreign' ex-soldiers, the truth is at once more complicated and more disturbing.

The sequel to the memo is instructive. Three weeks after Prescott-Decie's report, his fellow Munster divisional commissioner, Lieutenant-Colonel Gerald

THE FREEMAN'S JOURNAL SATURDAY, JULY 10, 1920.   5

SENSATIONAL POLICE DEVELOPMENTS IN KERRY

REFUSAL TO OBEY ORDERS

Fourteen Listowel Constables Stand Against Divisional Commissioner

MR. SMYTH'S STARTLING SPEECH

Police Threat of Bloody Resistance if Arrest Attempted

A most sensational report of disaffection in the ranks of the R.I.C. comes from Listowel, Co. Kerry.

According to an account circulated in the "Irish Bulletin," fourteen members of the force have decidedly refused to carry out orders given by Mr. Smyth, Divisional Commissioner for Munster.

On June 17, it is alleged, the police in occupation of the barracks were instructed to hand over the premises to the military. This they refused to do.

On the following day County Inspector O'Shee visited the barracks. Fourteen constables tendered their resignations as a result.

On June 19 a number of police and military appeared, headed by Mr. Smyth, who made a speech to the men, which, according to the report given, was of a most extraordinary character.

The spokesman of the constables, at the conclusion, protested vehemently against Mr. Smyth's remarks, and threw off his cap, belt, and side-arms.

His arrest was at once ordered, whereupon his collegues threatened that the room would "run red with blood" if a hand was laid upon him.

No statement relating to the affair could be obtained from the Castle last night.

STATEMENT BY DISAFFECTED CONSTABLES

Several constables who were present during the extraordinary episode at Listowel have made a statement for publication, and are ready to attest its truth.

16. The *Freeman's Journal's* report on the 'Listowel mutiny', provoked by a pep talk by RIC Munster divisional commissioner Lieutenant-Colonel Gerald Smyth, in the presence of his superior, General Tudor (right). According to Smith, 'You may make mistakes and innocent persons may be shot but that cannot be helped'. (Freeman's Journal, 10 July 1920, and Garda Archives)

MAJOR GENERAL H.H.TUDOR
Inspector General Royal Irish Constabulary
1920-1

Smyth, delivered a pep talk to disgruntled police constables in Listowel, County Kerry. As his superior General Tudor looked on, Smyth urged his men to move aggressively against civilians and to shoot anyone whom they considered suspicious. His remarks echoed the sentiments expressed by Prescott-Decie: 'You may make mistakes and innocent persons may be shot but that cannot be helped and you are bound to get the right parties some time. The more you shoot, the better I will like you, and I assure you no policeman will get into trouble for shooting any man.'

But Smyth's speech aroused violent opposition from his constables, who evicted both Smyth and Tudor from their barracks and threatened to physically resist an attempt to arrest their spokesman, Constable Jeremiah Mee. When those constables told their stories to the *Freeman's Journal* (an account verified by a number of those present), British politicians scrambled to refute the charges. As the Prescott-Decie memo shows, however, the denial of the 'Listowel mutiny' charges was a dissembling exercise by senior members of the British cabinet, displaying a cynical dishonesty that not only characterised its efforts in Ireland generally during 1920–21 but also drove its military leaders to distraction. The publication of his Listowel speech proved as fatal for Smyth as he had hoped its utterance would be for republicans in Kerry. A month later, on 17 July 1920, he was enjoying a drink in the smoking room of the Cork Conservative Club. Guided by a sympathetic porter, six IRA gunmen burst into the room and shot him dead, as the one-armed war veteran struggled to draw his pistol. Smyth's assassination shook Dublin Castle and sparked anti-Catholic riots in his native Banbridge.

Prescott-Decie remained a leading figure in the RIC and in late 1920 was promoted to senior commissioner for Munster, effectively heading RIC efforts in the martial law area for the remainder of the conflict. After the war he became active in unionist politics, but was ultimately disgraced by his later involvement in the British fascist movement. As is the way of things, history has proved far kinder to the reputations of Winston Churchill and David Lloyd George, who secretly authorised, yet publicly denied, the policy so memorably outlined by Prescott-Decie in that fateful summer of 1920.

Chapter 5

Who were the Black and Tans?

W.J. Lowe

W hen the republican campaign against the RIC and others thought sympathetic to Dublin Castle became more violent and successful in late 1919, the police abandoned hundreds of rural facilities to consolidate shrinking ranks in fewer, fortified stations. The pressure exerted directly on RIC men, their families, friends and those who did business with them resulted in unfilled vacancies from casualties, resignations and retirements.

Lloyd George's government could not recognise the IRA or Dáil Éireann as belligerents and insisted that counter-insurgency was 'a policeman's job supported by the military and not *vice versa*', which placed responsibility squarely on the RIC. The role of the RIC as a largely domestic police force with strong community ties had been steadily compromised since 1916 by more aggressive tactics against nationalists and heavier reliance on the military. Faced with the need for more, better-prepared men wearing police uniforms, the government augmented RIC numbers and capabilities by recruiting Great War veterans from throughout the UK. From early 1920 through to the Truce in July 1921, 13,732 new police recruits were added to the nearly 10,000 members of the 'old' RIC to maintain a constabulary strength that, at the end, reached about 14,500.

The new recruits stood out in RIC ranks anyway, but an initial shortage of complete bottle-green constabulary uniforms resulted in the temporary issue of military khaki and the name that stuck: the 'Black and Tans'. The Black and Tans were sworn as constables to reinforce county stations and their experience with weapons and tactics gave the RIC a tougher edge. The IRA campaign led to another recruitment initiative in July 1920, the Auxiliary Division (ADRIC) or 'Auxies', former military officers who wore distinctive Tam o' Shanter caps and operated in counter-insurgency units independent of other RIC formations.

Even though the Auxiliaries were a separate category of police, they were often combined under the shorthand of 'Black and Tans'. They were never regarded as ordinary Irish constables, by the communities in which they served or by other policemen, and are popularly remembered for brutality and the militarisation of the police. There is substance to the popular characterisation. The Black and Tans, and the Auxiliaries especially, were part of the escalation

17. Black and Tans inspection.

of violence in Ireland in 1920–21, and they are inseparable from reprisals against civilians. Indeed, it is hard to imagine the RIC executing a systematic reprisal policy without them. The Black and Tans and Auxiliaries helped to destroy residual community support for the RIC. But who were the nearly 14,000 men who joined the RIC ranks as irregulars?

A personnel register was maintained at Headquarters in Dublin Castle. The original manuscript ledgers are preserved in the Public Records Office (PRO), Kew (HO 184), and include all policemen recruited between 1816 and disbandment in 1922, including Black and Tans and Auxiliaries. RIC record-keeping was meticulous. Complete, consistent information on individual police careers is available at least until 1919.

The records for men recruited to the RIC from early 1920 are not as complete as those kept for the previous century. Enrolments and departures during the Black and Tan era occurred at a much higher rate, and other work generated by the War of Independence taxed RIC staff resources. Entries for Black and Tan constables are, generally, more complete than those for Auxiliaries.

The leanness of information for Auxiliaries suggests that more detailed information was kept elsewhere and/or there was a disinclination to keep accessible records about a counter-terror group. There is one reference to a 'secret file'. Still, the register contains important information about the men who joined the RIC as both Black and Tans and Auxiliaries. A twenty per cent sample (every fifth entry) of all those who joined the new RIC beginning in 1920 furnishes a representative population of 2,745 cases—2,302 Black and Tans and 443 Auxiliaries.

A recruitment system for the new units was set up throughout the UK. One third (916) of all sampled recruits joined in London. Another thirty-six per cent (990) were recruited in Liverpool and Glasgow. Nearly fourteen per cent of recruitment transactions occurred in Ireland. Folk memory holds that the British administration was not very concerned about the backgrounds of Black and Tan recruits, as long as they had military experience. An RIC constable who staffed the London office recalled that 'a canard has been put about that we recruited criminals deliberately . . . We had a police report on every candidate and accepted no man whose army character was assessed at less than "good"'. Douglas Duff, a Black and Tan who wrote a memoir, recalled that 'it had not been hard' to join the RIC and that he was sent to Dublin the same day he was sworn in.

The Black and Tans and Auxiliaries were overwhelmingly British (78.6 per cent of the sample). Almost two thirds were English, fourteen per cent were Scottish, and fewer than five per cent came from Wales and outside the UK. An unexpected finding that is at odds with popular memory is that nearly nineteen per cent of the sampled recruits (514) were Irish-born, twenty per cent of Black and Tans and about ten per cent of Auxiliaries. Extrapolating from the sample, more than 2,300 of all Black and Tans and 225 of all Auxiliaries were Irish. Many Irishmen joined the RIC in a role assumed by folk memory to be the exclusive preserve of British mercenaries.

The information in the register cannot tell us why anyone joined the RIC at a time of intensifying violence. Douglas Duff, for example, was a twice-torpedoed former merchant seaman. Thankful to be alive, he spent a short time in a London monastery. He 'conceived the idea' of joining the RIC from newspaper accounts of the Irish conflict. 'That was on Monday morning—the following Friday, at dawn, I was steaming into Dublin Bay, with a rubber stamp mark on my arm that read "Royal Irish Constabulary".'

But Sebastian Barry, in his 1996 novel *The Whereabouts of Eneas McNulty*, convincingly imagines the difficult adjustments for unemployed veterans of the experience in the trenches. Eneas, from Sligo, is another unemployed merchant navy veteran who joins the RIC. He 'knows why there are places in the peelers when there are places nowhere else', but 'a fella must work'. As an Irish Black and Tan, he experiences 'the new world of guerilla war and reprisal, for a policeman is a target . . . Every recruited man is suspected by both sides of informing . . .' Eneas's decision earns him the lifelong enmity of Sligo republicans and, decades later, he becomes the last RIC casualty. Of the ADRIC Barry observed: 'Many of the Auxiliaries are decorated boys . . . and saw sights worse than the dreariest nightmares. And they have come back altered forever and in a way more marked by atrocity than honoured by medals. They are half nightmare themselves, in their uniforms patched together from Army and RIC stores.' The RIC, at least, offered a place for men with such experience, but Eneas was wary of being 'jostled in the very barracks by these haunted faces'.

Nineteenth- and early twentieth-century police records are rich sources of detailed information. The average age of the Black and Tans was 26.5 years and Auxiliaries were about three years older (29.4 years). Irish recruits were, on average, nearly a year and a half younger (25.5 years). The ten men who gave their birthplace as the USA were the tallest, at six feet, but the Irishmen maintained the constabulary height tradition at nearly five feet nine and a half inches, eight-tenths of an inch taller than other UK recruits.

Among the 490 Irish-born in the sample, nearly sixty per cent came from the provinces of Leinster (26.8 per cent) and Ulster (31.3 per cent). Munster and Connacht shared 37 per cent almost equally (the county of birth for almost five per cent is not known). Eighty-two per cent of Black and Tans and Auxiliaries sampled were Protestant, 17.4 per cent were Catholic and there were ten English Jews. The largest proportion of Catholics, not surprisingly, was found among the Irish recruits (fifty-nine per cent of the 478 Catholics in the sample).

Fifty-five per cent of the Irish recruits were Catholic, mostly concentrated among the Black and Tans. Those born in Connacht and Munster were overwhelmingly Catholic (both 78 per cent) and sixty per cent of the Leinster men were Catholic. Ulster-born Black and Tans were overwhelmingly Protestant (seventy-two per cent). The forty-six Irish Auxiliaries included seventeen Catholics.

Service in these forces attracted single men. Only twenty-five per cent of the recruits were married, with the Irish the least likely (12.1 per cent) and Scots most likely (31.8 per cent) to be married. Under the 'old' RIC *Code*, only single men were enrolled among the rank-and-file, who had to wait seven years for permission to marry. It is a measure of the seriousness of the security situation that married men were recruited at all. Besides being younger, Irish Black and Tans were probably less likely to be married because of risks to their families.

Two categories of prior occupations were recorded for Black and Tans. One hundred and eighty distinct occupations that cover the range of UK industries have been identified in the sample, all but a few of which were held by Black-and-Tans. More than a third of Black and Tan occupations can be grouped into several categories, the largest of which are clerks (4.3 per cent), agriculture (6.7 per cent), labourers (14.4 per cent), mechanics (2.6 per cent), and railway employees (4.5 per cent). Only 136 of the Black and Tans in the sample were recruited directly from military service. Second occupations are listed for almost sixty-eight per cent of those in the sample and 1,802 of those men (over sixty-five per cent of the entire sample) were military veterans. ADRIC men, on the other hand, generally showed only one occupation: 'former military officer', which accounted for nearly ninety-five per cent of the sample.

While seventy per cent of English and over eighty per cent of Scots Black and Tans had prior military service, fewer than forty per cent of Irish recruits were veterans. Irishmen *without* prior military service continued to join the RIC. Clearly, unemployment forged a previously unseen connection with RIC recruiting traditions among the Irish-born Black and Tans. Dublin Castle would have quietly recognised them as the backbone of the future RIC, but publicity would invite IRA intimidation of recruits and their families.

The Black and Tans, with their military experience, received cursory training at the RIC depot in Dublin's Phoenix Park before being posted to stations throughout Ireland. The register contains information on the postings of only fifty-four per cent of those in the sample, mostly about Black and Tans. But the data appear to reliably represent deployments because their known first postings correspond very closely to the counties in which RIC records (PRO, CO 904/148) show both large numbers of incidents and RIC casualties. Forty-eight per cent of Black and Tan reinforcements for whom postings are known went to the six counties where IRA activity against the police was heaviest.

The most dangerous county for the RIC was Cork, where at least 119 policemen were wounded and ninety killed. Cork also received the largest number of Black and Tan reinforcements—eleven per cent of the total or (extrapolating from the sample) more than 1,500 police irregulars. Close behind was Tipperary, with less than eleven per cent of Black and Tan assignments, or just under 1,500 men. More than 1,000 Black and Tans appear to have been sent to Galway. When Limerick, Clare and Kerry are added, these six counties received more than 6,600 of all the Black and Tans deployed.

All of the Black and Tans were not stationed in the southern and south-western counties at the same time, but they must have been very noticeable additions in small communities, another reason why they were remembered so vividly. The accompanying map also demonstrates that assignments to other counties varied widely and, for example, many fewer Black and Tans were needed to supplement the Ulster special constabularies.

The Black and Tans had a reputation for violent indiscipline that could be very dangerous to Irish civilians and even other policemen. Members of the 'old' RIC had very mixed reactions to their presence and violent behaviour that not all officers were able to restrain. Black and Tans were thought of as 'gun-happy' and the Auxiliaries' ferocity was reputed to be fuelled by heavy drinking. Even officers who regarded the Black and Tans as effective assets against the

Do You Want a Job?

YOU CAN JOIN THE R.I.C.

"The Finest Constabulary Force in the World."

PAY - -   10/- Daily ; Temporary Bonus 12/- weekly for Married Men, 6/- weekly for Single Men, in addition. Service Pay is also issuable in certain cases—1/- and 2/- a day.

UNIFORM - - -   Free to all Recruits ; Boot Allowances of 1/6 per week extra.

QUARTERS - - -   Free Subsistence Allowance in addition when away from station, on duty.

LEAVE - - - - -   A Month's Leave on Full Pay every twelve months. A Free Railway Warrant from Ireland to your home and back.

PENSIONS - - -   Pensions on the Highest Scale payable to any police force in the United Kingdom.

PROMOTION - -   Opportunities for Men of special ability occur frequently

COMPENSATION   For wounds received in action generous Compensation is paid

If you have the Physique--If you have a Good Character
And especially--If you are an Ex-Service Man

You can join the R.I.C. to-day.

Call at any Army Recruiting Office or write to, or call at, either of the following Addresses

LONDON:	LIVERPOOL:	GLASGOW:	DUBLIN:
The Recruiting H.Q., Great Scotland Yard, S.W.I.	The Recruiting Office, 19, Old Haymarket.	The Recruiting Office, 130, Bath Street.	Commandant R.I.C. Depot, Phœnix Park.

❡ REMEMBER   IF YOU DON'T LIKE THE JOB—YOU CAN GIVE A MONTH'S NOTICE—AND LEAVE.

18. A recruitment poster for the police reinforcements later known as 'Black and Tans'.

IRA acknowledged that the strict disciplinary system in the RIC *Code* had not anticipated a large number of men who were not trained as policemen.

The military-trained reinforcements were supposed to enable the RIC to suppress the armed Irish independence movement. But incidents rose steeply and simultaneously with the introduction of the Black and Tans and Auxiliaries until the Truce. The new recruits showed initial enthusiasm for the work, but the realities of wartime Ireland soon bore in. During the twelve months prior to the Truce, 330 members of the RIC were killed. The register indicates that 147 (forty-five per cent) of these deaths were among Black and Tans and Auxiliaries, a large share of the dangerous duty and casualties. Also, life in crowded, isolated stations (including attempts to impose discipline), boredom and community hostility diminished the appeal of good pay.

The RIC was disbanded after the Anglo-Irish Treaty of December 1921, but only thirty-nine per cent of the sample (perhaps a total of 5,550 men) were still in the force to be mustered out in 1922. Irish recruits, despite the dangers, were much more likely than those from Britain (fifty-five per cent compared to thirty-six per cent of the English and thirty-nine per cent of the Scots) to be in the RIC at disbandment. The register is incomplete for 35.6 per cent (almost 4,900) of Black and Tans and Auxiliaries and we do not know how they separated from the RIC. But the information in the sample for those who left but were not disbanded is probably a good indication. Dismissals, rarely with details, accounted for 128 of separations, which suggests termination for almost 650 Black and Tan and ADRIC recruits. Sixty-one men are reported in the ambiguous category 'discharged'. The most common termination of service prior to disbandment was resignation.

The register contains reasons for only sixteen per cent of those who resigned, which is consistent with the promise in the enlistment poster: 'If you don't like the job—you can give a month's notice—and leave'. But there were several themes. Some claimed ill health, while about 120 gave reasons related to personal affairs. Just over thirty English and Scots policemen were dissatisfied with the work, a reason that caused only one Irishman to resign. Nearly seventy English and Scots in the sample left to take a better position, an option available to only ten Irishmen. A reason for resignation cited only by Irishmen is intimidation of family members (ten, or two per cent of the Irish in the sample), which suggests that 100 Irishmen may have resigned to protect loved ones.

It was not coincidental that resignations among the Black and Tans increased along with the tedium of life under siege, violence and casualties. Douglas Duff probably summed up the view of the men who resigned and went home pretty well: 'Remember, we were mercenary soldiers fighting for our pay, not patriots willing and anxious to die for our country . . . Our job was to earn our pay by suppressing armed rebellion, not to die in some foolish . . . "forlorn hope".' Even though the dehumanising experience of the First World War was assumed to have hardened Black and Tans and Auxiliaries, sanctioned reprisals against Irish civilians did not sit well with all of the new recruits. Duff recalled 'official reprisals' as 'horrible and dastardly burning of houses and furniture' with the 'due force of the law'.

When the RIC disbanded in 1922, all of those still enrolled, including Black and Tans and Auxiliaries, were given lifetime annuities (later converted to indexed pensions). The ADRIC entries are almost entirely blank, but the Black and Tan entries are much more complete. Disbandment annuities were based on length of service, with the longest service possible about two years. The annual payment for each man varied between £55 for those who served longest and £47 for the most recent recruits. The average payment for each Black-and-Tan in the sample was £52. Irish Black and Tans averaged annuities of £55, higher than the English (£51.3) or Scots (£49.8) because more Irishmen remained in the RIC until the end.

The militarisation of the RIC through the recruitment of veterans ultimately failed. Violence actually increased along with Black and Tan deployment, and the heavily reinforced RIC only achieved a stand-off with the IRA. The remaining Black and Tan and ADRIC policemen left in 1922 and the 'old' RIC went with them. The association of the Black and Tans with violence and intimidation against civilians established their reputation. Specific responsibility for reprisals is difficult to attribute, but tradition blames the Black and Tans for indiscriminate violence that had not been associated with the 'old' RIC. Military experience in the trenches seems to have made them the right men for Lloyd George's 'policeman's job'.

Despite the record and legend of their RIC service, the personal details of Black and Tans and Auxiliaries emphasise that they were not remarkable among British workingmen and war veterans, except that they were willing to take a chance on dangerous duty in Ireland. But the untold story is the surprising number of young Irishmen who joined the RIC in its final months, despite the dangers for themselves and their families. Most Irish Black and Tans had not served in the military but, through it all, were the most likely to be serving at disbandment. Why did Irishmen join the RIC in the Black and Tan era and how did they escape notice for eighty years?

Until 1919 the Irish police service was considered decently paid, pensioned employment and an attractive alternative to emigration. But did more than 2,000 Irishmen find employment and emigration prospects so discouraging in 1920–1 that, like Eneas McNulty, even the embattled RIC was attractive? Good wages in a time of high unemployment were an inducement. But, still, it is a testament to the post-war environment that so many risked being on the 'wrong side' in the War of Independence.

It is perhaps easier to conjecture about why so many Irish Black and Tans went unnoticed. Neither the policemen nor their families would have been eager to call attention to their belated RIC service during or after the War of Independence. RIC men were not posted to their home counties and policemen had little contact with the communities in which they were stationed during 1920–1, so it is possible that the recruits were able to blend in with members of the 'old' RIC. Still, that there were so many Irishmen among the Black and Tans shows that there is still much to learn about the complexities of the War of Independence.

Acknowledgements
The author wishes to thank Michelle Sheldon, Jerold Davis and Jessica McLaughlin for their assistance.

Chapter 6

Revolutionary justice: the Dáil Éireann courts

Mary Kotsonouris

'This is the golden hour. Therefore be prepared.' Thus did Austin Stack admonish the District Registrars throughout Ireland when, on 9 August 1921, he sent them detailed instructions on the procedures and regulations of the Dáil courts. No one was left in any doubt where the real authority lay: henceforth the parish and district courts were to be directly under the control of his Ministry. 'Once the courts are established,' Stack told the West Donegal Registrar, 'Comhairle Ceantair have no authority over them (apart from helping litigants make contact or to boycott enemy courts) but otherwise courts and court officials are completely under the jurisdiction of the Minister for Home Affairs and no other person has authority over them.'

A team of organisers—about ten men in all—were employed by the ministry on a full-time basis and were assigned to specific areas: they supervised the election of justices, instructed the clerks in their duties and sent weekly reports back to headquarters. They had access to the local TDs and IRA brigade officers and they were Stack's eyes and ears in assessing the performance of the courts in every locality. Once established, the registrar was responsible for the operation of the courts in each parliamentary constituency which had its own District Court with a complement of five judges, of whom three were a bench. They were chosen by the parish justices. The latter, in turn, were elected by a convention comprising Sinn Féin, trades councils, members of the rural or urban authorities, the Irish Volunteers and Cumann na mBan. While clergymen of any denomination were *ex officio* deemed to be eligible, it was more often that not the Catholic curate who presided at the parish court. These parish courts were central to the acceptability of the system.

The justices were representative of the local people, and, therefore, answerable to them in a way a Resident Magistrate (RM) could never be. It was considered a great honour to be elected, and for the most part, they appear to have taken their duties seriously and were at pains to stress their judicial independence. Many litigants who were unsuccessful in their suit or who had fines levied against them were quick to complain to the Ministry and thus furnish future students with a wealth of information on the public response to this innovation. Whatever its faults—and they were many—the parish court provided a cheap

19. *Republican Court 1921* by Seán Keating.

and immediate access to justice and, moreover, it was 'consumer driven' in a way no court could possibly be today. Dáil Éireann was anxious to attract to its own departments users of those services provided by the British administration and none more than to its courts. Stack, therefore, responded to many complaints by lengthy investigations and frequently seemed to interfere inappropriately in several instances. How did he came to have such a system of courts to preside over in the first place, even before the cessation of hostilities and the truce? How could there exist an alternative judicial framework when he was only then in a position to furnish it with rules of procedure?

In a story studded with paradoxes, the most striking paradox was that the 'Dáil courts' were not established by Dáil Éireann! The breakaway from the British or statutory courts had been made by separate communities but occurred almost spontaneously throughout the country in the previous year. While Griffith preached a self-governing administration of justice from 1905 and made it part of Sinn Féin policy, the Dáil had taken few practical steps in its first year, apart from passing a decree in August 1919 to set up a system of 'National Arbitration Courts' which amounted to little more than an aspiration. The foundation, on which Stack built, had its roots in the agrarian disturbances in the west, where smallholders, impatient with the procedures of the Congested District Boards, and often reinforced by gangs of disaffected men, took advantage of the generally unsettled conditions to force landowners out of their property by terrorising them. Such lawlessness threatened to overshadow the confident expectations and national pride engendered by the victory of Sinn Féin candidates in the general election of 1918 and the subsequent creation of Dáil Éireann. It became necessary to take urgent steps to prevent a conflagration, so local leaders in the community set up ad hoc tribunals to which disputes could be referred and settled with some degree of rough justice.

Conor Maguire—later to be a Chief Justice—who was then practising as a solicitor in Mayo wrote a first-hand account of this development in the *Capuchin Annual* in 1968. Similar tribunals sprang up in several places and at the same time, the newspapers were reporting another phenomenon of self-policing. Groups of Volunteers took on themselves the role of village constable, 'arresting' persons who breached the peace or stole property: they even investigated crimes which were reported to them and began to conduct trials. The *Freeman's Journal* of 4 June 1920 reviewed the work of the Volunteer patrols in twenty-one counties over the previous six weeks: it included dispelling a riot, punishing culprits for damage to property and recovering the proceeds of bank and post-office robberies. They regularly policed race meetings and fair days. All of this was the subject of much comment not only in the House of Commons, but in the British and foreign press. In May 1920 the operation of the Land Courts was brought under the control of the Ministry of Agriculture and in the same month, Austin Stack circulated, by means of the Sinn Féin Clubs, details of a scheme for agreed arbitration procedures to be organised in districts and parishes. Meetings were held to elect judges and throughout that summer, proceedings were reported in the local newspapers under the heading 'Sinn Féin Arbitration Court'.

However, matters were brought a step further the following month when, on 29 June, Dáil Éireann issued a decree establishing 'Courts of Justice and Equity' and authorising the Ministry of Home Affairs to establish courts having a criminal jurisdiction. While there is no explanation for the rapidity of the transition from one system to another, the Minister is reported as saying that the Arbitration Courts depended on the consent of both parties but that the country was in such a state at the present time that the people looked to the republican government for their law and equity and in a very short time they would have ousted the English courts altogether. It was therefore necessary to take immediate steps to set up courts throughout the country which would be competent to hear every class of case similar to the cases dealt with in English Courts of Petty Sessions and Courts of County Sessions and Assize so far as civil jurisdiction was concerned.

In other words, the courts were to be organised nationally under the immediate authority of the Dáil, they would correspond in jurisdiction to the courts established by statute and their decisions would be enforced by sanctions, if necessary. However, another year would pass before the ideal could be fully realised. Although a committee of lawyers met to draft the constitution and rules of the courts—the judiciary—and four professional judges were appointed (with considerable optimism, 'for life'), the state of the country worsened and imposed considerable restraints on Stack's plans.

In the meantime the so-called 'enemy' courts had also been adversely affected by the events of the previous year. There were over 600 justices of the peace, many of them dignitaries in local councils, the majority having nationalist sympathies. A large number had resigned their commissions when the conflict started or refused to serve on the Petty Sessions. The Resident Magistrates, who held their office at the pleasure of the Lord Lieutenant, were salaried officials and were mostly former military or police officers who were traditionally distrusted by the Irish people. As political violence increased, the RIC had to withdraw to barracks for their own safety, and under martial law, Crimes Courts or courts martial were set up to handle most offences, because witnesses refused to give evidence in the regular court; there were frequent press reports of Resident Magistrates adjourning the Petty Sessions because there were no cases to be heard. It was the same story with the Quarter Sessions which had jurisdiction to hear criminal matters before a jury. The few jurymen who might be minded to attend were turned back on the road by the IRA. When the judges of the High Court went out on the Assizes the courthouses were protected by sandbags and barbed wire and ringed by soldiers with fixed bayonets. Mr Justice Pim complained in Galway 'that the control of the country and the law had become so weakened as to make it no longer possible to carry on'. However, with weary courage, the judges carried on as best they could but,

20. A republican court sitting in Westport, Co. Mayo.

increasingly, in courthouses emptied of all save lawyers, officials and police. Only in Dublin were they able to sit in conditions approaching normality.

Strangely enough, it was only in Dublin also that the professional judges of Dáil Éireann were able to hold their courts as soon as the rules on procedure had been settled. James Creed Meredith KC and Arthur Clery, Professor of Law at UCD, had been appointed to the Supreme Court of the Republic: Stack also secured the services of Cahir Davitt and Diarmuid Crowley—both of whom had been called to the Bar as recently as 1916—to act as Circuit Judges. However, by September 1920, martial law had been proclaimed over several areas and the Dáil courts suppressed, but all four still managed to hold some sittings in Dublin. The Circuit Judges were anxious to get down the country and eventually, in November 1920, persuaded Stack to allow them go. No communication was possible between the Ministry and the Court Registrars by that time, so all arrangements would have to be made in situ and be liable to change at the last moment to avoid arrest. Crowley went to the west and was arrested within weeks: he was sentenced to two years' hard labour by a court martial. Davitt, although he had many close encounters, not only managed to slip through the military net, but to hold makeshift courts in at least five counties during the 'Terror', as the period between October 1920 and March 1921 is referred to in correspondence.

By the following June, communication was resumed with headquarters and the Minister was demanding reports and returns from all the registrars for the previous eight months. He was determined that during the period of the truce, the courts would become so entrenched that no matter the outcome of any talks, the structures would be strong enough to survive—hence his rallying call to the registrars. He judged the situation rightly: although there were several confrontations with the RIC and an angry rebuke from Lloyd George to Griffith and Collins on the first day of the London conference, the Dáil courts took on a tremendous amount of new business, especially from commercial companies and local authorities. This growth was threatened by the Treaty, and particularly by the proclamation of 16 January 1922 which stated that the law courts and all public bodies formerly under the authority of the British government were to continue in operation until the establishment of the Irish Free State.

There was consternation and a clamour that the Dáil courts should not be abandoned. Reassurance was immediately to hand. George Nicholls TD, a solicitor from Galway, was given the sole task of supervising the courts as an assistant minister in the Provisional Government. He wrote to the protesting registrars and justices:

'As the republic and the republican government still stands, orders and instructions issued by the Provisional Government have no influence in any way on republican court officials. The republican courts shall continue to function as heretofore and all necessary steps must be taken to boycott the enemy courts until the Irish people approve of the Free State government. Our position remains unchanged and the republican courts are the only legal courts of the Irish people'.

Around the time of this strange advice, the same junior minister considered whether he should prepare the commissions for his majesty's judges to be sent on the winter assizes. After consideration over several days they were not permitted to go, probably because it proved impossible to remove from the wording of the commission the status of the king vis-à-vis his Irish subjects.

So the Dáil courts continued to prosper at the expense of those which alone were recognised under the terms of the Anglo-Irish treaty. Outside of Dublin most serious crimes were tried before a Dáil circuit judge sitting with a jury. Convicted prisoners served their sentences in the state gaols. The republican police had a brigade in each area, attended at the courts and executed their warrants and judgements, although there were ample grounds for complaint in the haphazard fashion in which the latter duties were carried out. The Royal Irish Constabulary was being stood down and the formation of the Garda Síochána was bogged down in continuing controversy. Debtors frequently sought injunctions to stop plaintiffs suing them in the established courts, whose orders sheriffs were slow to execute in any case. Resident Magistrates and their clerks protested to the Chief Secretary's Office that their courthouses had been taken over by the Parish Courts, but nothing was done about it and they finally gave up.

The matter of the dual jurisdiction did not trouble the government unduly: when it was raised in cabinet discussion was deferred. However, a memorandum was prepared—probably by Hugh Kennedy, the legal adviser—that the high and county courts should be given back the work that had been taken from them by the Dáil supreme and circuit courts and that lawyers should replace the Resident Magistrates in reformed petty sessions. Although the drafting of the Free State constitution had been completed, it was not suggested that a committee should begin immediately to plan for the new courts to be established under it. Such a move would, at least, have given the impression that something was being done to sort out the muddle. The drift continued until 23 June 1922 when the Law Adviser was instructed to prepare commissions for the summer assizes, although there was no hint of what cases were to be heard, nor from what venues accused persons could be returned for trial. The unspoken questions remained unanswered because five days later the Civil War broke out. On 13 July 1922, the assistant minister, purporting to act under a decision of the 'Dáil Éireann Cabinet', suspended the sitting of the supreme court and ordered the immediate return of the judges from their circuits. When George Plunkett, a republican prisoner, obtained a conditional order of *Habeas Corpus* from Judge Crowley, the government, on 25 July, hastily rescinded the decree of 29 June 1920 which had created the Dáil courts, leaving only the parish and district courts outside of Dublin in place until some alternative form of summary justice was devised.

The reaction that greeted the proclamation of the previous January was revived in the astonished protests, resolutions of county councils and letters to the papers. It later became clear that the Provisional Government and its advisers had no appreciation of the extent or nature of the work carried on in the courts, nor the chaos that would follow from the unheralded suppression. Although the official statement laid heavy emphasis on the immediate availability of an alternative legal system which was now under native rule and paid for by the taxpayer, it was not in a state of readiness, partly because the goalposts had been moved. There were no courts to which offenders could

21. Arthur Griffiths.

be sent for trial, nor juries willing to serve. The county courts had practically ground to a halt and there was no possibility that the assize judges could travel while civil war raged. The transition was easier in Dublin where there truly was an entire hierarchy of courts in working order. Sir James Molony, the Lord Chief Justice, wrote to Hugh Kennedy on 15 July 1922—a full week before the recession of the 1920 Decree—anticipating that there would be a 'considerable influx of business into these courts now that the republican courts had been brought to an end'; at the same time he conceded that the title 'Rialtas Sealadach na hÉireann' ('Provisional Government of Ireland') would appear in future on the documents of the High Court. Almost two years would pass before Molony ceased to the Lord Chief Justice of Ireland, a title he jealously guarded in spite of the Government of Ireland Act 1920. The Resident Magistrates were pensioned off to be replaced by twenty-seven male lawyers in October, tactfully called 'District Justices'. At the same time, a committee was appointed under Lord Glenavy—a former Lord Chief Justice and Lord Chancellor, now Chairman of Seanad Éireann—to advise on the structures and form of the future constitutional courts. The resulting bill took more than eight months to pass through the Dáil and Seanad.

In an impressive ceremony at Dublin Castle on 11 June 1924, Hugh Kennedy, now Chief Justice of the Irish Free State, administered the oath of office to his eight fellow judges. Four of them had held judicial office under the British but also included was Justice Meredith, formerly president of the Dáil supreme court. He had sat for the last time that day as Chief Judicial Commissioner in the Dáil Éireann Courts Winding up Commission in the upper yard of the castle The latter had been established by statute in August 1923 to adjudicate and register more than five thousand Dáil court judgements left in the air when the courts were suppressed. The commission was given extraordinary, though temporary, judicial powers which were transferred to the High Court in 1925. This jurisdiction continued to be actively exercised well into the following decade. It has frequently been remarked that the legal system which emerged in independent Ireland was a mirror image of that in England: however, the circuit and district Courts were modelled directly on those of Dáil Éireann. Wigs and gowns and judicial titles were retained but many lawyers prominently associated with the seditious courts were appointed to the bench, mostly notably, Conor Maguire, Chief Justice, and Cahir Davitt, President of the High Court. In a judgement issued in January 1923 the Land Court had been declared an illegal and usurping tribunal: by 1925 its judgements were being upheld in the High Court by Justice Wylie, who had prosecuted at the court martial of the leaders of the 1916 Rising. The way it turned out was a fine example of an Irish solution to an Irish problem.

Chapter 7

'Pilgrimville': the Templemore miracles, 1920

John Reynolds

On the night of 16 August 1920 'wild scenes were witnessed' in Templemore, County Tipperary, as the Northamptonshire Regiment carried out reprisals following the killing of RIC District Inspector William Wilson by the IRA. According to a local press report, 'soldiers joined in the outbreak . . . volleys were fired, houses attacked, shops looted, the town hall was burned down, and three creameries destroyed'. (Ironically, two members of the regiment, Captain S. H. Beattie MC and Lance Corporal H. J. Fuggle, were to lose their lives in the fire.)

Immediately after these deaths, reports of 'supernatural manifestations, accompanied by cures', in Templemore and also in the townland of Curraheen, near the village of Gortagarry, appeared in local and national newspapers. It was alleged that religious statues at several premises, including the RIC barracks in Templemore, were shedding tears of blood. It was reported that local farm labourer James Walsh was experiencing Marian apparitions, and that a 'holy well' had appeared in his bedroom floor. The *Tipperary Star* reported that 'after the outburst on Monday night some of the statues from which blood had been oozing were taken by Walsh to Templemore, and it is believed that it was this that saved the town from destruction'. The *Limerick Leader* reported that 'prominent townsmen assembled around the bleeding statues and offered prayers aloud, thanking God that the town was saved on Monday night, and that none of the inoffensive people of Templemore suffered any casualties'. Some believed that divine intervention had prevented the town from being completely destroyed in revenge for the death of DI Wilson, and that 'Our Lady had saved Templemore'.

On 31 August 1920, RIC County Inspector Dunlop reported to Dublin Castle that 'on 20th inst. miraculous apparitions are alleged to have appeared in Templemore and Curraheen. Sacred statues belonging to a man named Walsh and a constable Wimsey stationed at Templemore are alleged to have begun to bleed, and several miraculous cures are said to have taken place.' By 4 September Dunlop estimated that more than 15,000 persons per day were making the pilgrimage to Templemore and onwards to Curraheen. Dunlop removed the statue from the barracks and placed it with other statues on an improvised altar that had been erected in a yard beside Dwan's shop. This followed an incident during which the barracks was besieged by a large crowd of pilgrims anxious to see the bleeding statue. People entered the barracks and had to be forcibly removed by the RIC. Wimsey left the police shortly afterwards, reportedly to 'join a religious order'. Dunlop told Dublin Castle that the alleged miracles were having a positive effect on the locality, describing the conduct of the large crowds as 'exemplary'. Templemore was referred to as 'Pilgrimville' or 'Pilgrimstown' by newspapers, and to cater for the thousands of pilgrims categorised by newspapers as 'the halt, the maim and the blind', additional trains originating from Kingsbridge Station in Dublin were added to the normal schedule. Revd Collier, a correspondent for the *Catholic Times*, visited Templemore and estimated that 6,000 to 8,000 people were at Dwan's, many of them having been there overnight. He saw four statues, each with blood trickling down the face, neck, breasts and body.

The alleged visionary, James Walsh, was aged sixteen at the time of these events and was described as a 'simple-mannered youth' and a 'saint if ever there was one'. He told journalists that he had spent time in the Cistercian monastery in Roscrea as a novice, leaving because of ill-health, but intended 'to enter a religious order'. Walsh became an instant celebrity, and within days advertising had appeared in newspapers offering for sale 'photographs of the boy to whom

22. The improvised altar that had been erected in a yard beside Dwan's shop, Templemore, 22 August 1920. (National Photographic Archive)

the blessed virgin appeared'. Pilgrims visiting Templemore travelled on to the cottage at Curraheen where Walsh lived, also regarded as a place of pilgrimage because of the reported existence of a holy well. The throng of pilgrims prompted one elderly visitor to make an analogy with the Alaskan gold rush of 1897–8, remarking that "twas easier to get from Skagway to the Klondike' than from Templemore to Curraheen. Walsh told journalists that he had started to experience Marian apparitions in August and that statues in his bedroom began to move and shed tears of blood. Acting on instructions from the Virgin Mary, he dug a hole in his bedroom floor from which a holy well appeared, 'producing a great volume of water'.

As reports of the apparitions and miracles spread, the number of pilgrims increased. Many people claimed to have been healed either by direct contact with Walsh or by exposure to the bleeding statues or crucifix. Some visitors were not convinced, however, and one journalist wrote that he came 'to see a miracle and saw one. It was not a miracle of bleeding statues but of pathetic belief'. The *Limerick Leader* reported the case of former soldier Martin Monahan, the first person claiming to have been cured by Walsh. Monahan had spent three years in the military hospital at Richmond Barracks with shrapnel injuries. He claimed to have entered Dwan's yard on crutches but left 'with full use of his limbs' after Walsh had touched his legs with one of the statues. Other well-publicised cases included those of a Miss Guerin and a Mr Gavin of Limerick, who were reportedly cured of 'paralysis' and 'acute hip disease' respectively.

The official position of the Catholic Church was one of 'extreme reserve', and at the height of the religious fervour that surrounded the miracles Bishop Fogarty of Limerick warned Mass-goers that 'they should restrain their judgement and not allow themselves to be carried away by excitement or popular rumour'. The parish priest of Templemore, Revd Kiely, refused to visit the statues, expressing the opinion that great caution needed to be exercised. Walsh travelled to other towns in the company of clergy, visiting Mount Mellary and Cashel, where he stayed as the guest of Monsignor Innocent Ryan. The *Irish Times* reported that statues and a crucifix in the presbytery in Cashel had begun to bleed when touched by Walsh, and as the news spread 'a piteous and clamorous crowd of invalids' arrived at the presbytery and requested that they be allowed to see and touch the statues that were on display outside the building. Monsignor Ryan wrote to the *Irish Times* in an attempt to stem the flow of pilgrims and to prevent events similar to those occurring at Templemore and Curraheen also taking place in Cashel.

Reporting the miracles to IRA GHQ, local vice-commandant Edward McGrath stated that the town was packed with 'pilgrims, beggars, stall-holders and undesirables. The police and military had disappeared off the streets and the IRA had taken over. They controlled traffic, introduced parking and restored order'. The IRA acted as stewards and marshals but did not appear on the streets in uniform. They took advantage of the absence of the military and police

23. James Walsh, the local farm labourer who claimed to have experienced Marian apparitions and to have discovered a 'holy well' in his bedroom floor. Within days advertising (right) had appeared in newspapers offering for sale 'photographs of the boy to whom the blessed virgin appeared'. (Tipperary Star, 4 September 1920)

from the streets to reconnoitre suitable locations for ambushes, and local IRA commander Jimmy Leahy imposed a levy of 2/6d per day on all cars bringing pilgrims from Templemore to Curraheen. Ostensibly the levy was imposed to pay for repairs to local roads that had been damaged by the throngs of pilgrims, and to pay the expenses of IRA men involved in traffic and crowd control duty. The imposition of the levy caused an outcry, and Count O'Byrne, Sinn Féin TD and chairman of North Tipperary County Council, met Leahy and pointed out that the levy was highly irregular. Leahy replied that 'everything had to be irregular to deal with the situation that had arisen'. The count suggested that the council should take over the collection of the levy but Leahy refused, saying that he intended to buy arms and ammunition with any balance left over after deducting the Volunteers' expenses. Pilgrims were reported to be loud in their praise of the 'splendid men of Óglaigh na hÉireann' (the Irish name for the Irish Volunteers was used to describe the IRA) who maintained order and prevented excessive profiteering by shopkeepers, caterers and hoteliers. Such activities were severely dealt with by the IRA, who imposed a scale of charges after 'due enquiry, deliberation and consideration of the abnormal conditions prevailing'. Collection boxes for the IRA and the republican womens organisation Cumann na mBan were placed along the pilgrimage route and this provided a substantial windfall for the IRA, with a total of £1,500 contributed, which was subsequently delivered to the brigade quartermaster.

Several days after the miracles began, Leahy and other IRA officers interrogated Walsh. They had started to view the 'whole business with incredulity', and were also seriously concerned that Volunteer discipline was being compromised. Pilgrims had begun to lavishly tip the IRA men, with the result that some Volunteers, who had previously been abstemious and enthusiastic, 'took to drink and began to forget that they were engaged in a life and death struggle for the country's freedom'. Walsh told Leahy that when he had conversed with the Virgin Mary she had indicated her approval of guerrilla tactics, including the shooting of Black and Tans, and wished to see the campaign intensified. Leahy and the others found it difficult 'to keep a straight face' and concluded that Walsh was either 'mentally abnormal or a hypocrite'. Leahy felt that the bizarre situation could not be allowed to continue, and also demanded that Walsh hand over some of the money that had been given to him by pilgrims. Walsh gave £75 to Leahy and this money was also passed to the quartermaster.

Following this meeting, Leahy visited Canon Ryan in Thurles and requested that the apparitions be denounced from the pulpit, thereby deterring pilgrims

24. Crowds milling about the entrance to Dwan's yard, 22 August 1920. (National Photographic Archive)

25. Michael Collins – ordered Dan Breen to contact 'the fellow who operates
the bleeding statue' and interview him. (Chrissy Osborne, *Michael Collins:
A Life in Pictures* [Mercier Press]).

from travelling to Templemore. Canon Ryan did not comply. Leahy also
contacted Michael Collins to express his concern about the detrimental effect
the situation was having on IRA operations. Collins ordered the prominent
Tipperary IRA leader Dan Breen to contact 'the fellow who operates the
bleeding statue' and interview him, to which Breen reluctantly agreed. Walsh
was taken to Dublin and interrogated by Breen, while Collins waited in the
next room. Breen reported back to Collins that Walsh 'was a fake', or possibly
even a spy, and his opinion was that the apparitions and miracles were not
genuine. Collins sarcastically replied, 'One can't take any notice of what you
say, Breen, because you have no religion'. Phil Shanahan, who owned a pub in
Dublin frequented by IRA members, was asked by Breen to drive the visionary
to Templemore, and that was the last Breen saw of the 'failure Walsh'. On
his return, Shanahan offered Breen water from the holy well at Curraheen to
drink, but Breen declined the offer. Having been rebuffed by Canon Ryan and
the Catholic Church, the IRA decided to resume the war in any case. On 29
September 1920 the IRA attacked a group of RIC men near Goldings Cross
RIC barracks, which was on the pilgrimage route between Templemore and
Curraheen. Constables Edward Noonan and Terence Flood were killed and
two others wounded. After the ambush, a group of pilgrims were stopped by

the IRA and forced to complete their journey with the 'dead bodies of the two policemen thrown across their knees in the car'.

As the IRA had intended, the ambush brought a substantial number of military and police reinforcements to the area, who engaged in a 'reign of terror by indulging in indiscriminate firing into houses and across fields'. The Northamptonshire Regiment went to the holy well at Curraheen and Dwan's yard in Templemore, where they removed crutches and other items left behind by pilgrims. Some soldiers decorated themselves with religious artefacts, while others feigned lameness and began using the crutches, parading the streets in mockery of the miracles. Rumours spread like wildfire that Templemore would be burned to the ground as a reprisal for the ambush, and pilgrims, stall-holders and tramps all made a hasty exit. Within twenty-four hours the town had returned to normality.

Michael Collins sent a courier to Tipperary to acquire one of the bleeding statues. Collins had received information from the local Catholic clergy that IRA Volunteers had engineered statues that would bleed at specific times. The internal mechanism of an alarm clock had been concealed inside the statue, connected to fountain pen inserts containing a mixture of sheep's blood and water. When the clock mechanism struck at certain times it would send a spurt of blood through the statue, giving the impression that it was bleeding. According to an eye-witness, Collins 'took hold of the statue and banged it off the side of the desk, and of course out fell the works of the alarm clock. "I knew it", he says. So that was the end of the bleeding statue.'

Shortly afterwards, local people heard that James Walsh had left for Australia. In 1947 he was granted Australian citizenship while living in Stawell, Victoria.

Chapter 8

Nationalism, empire and memory: the Connaught Rangers mutiny, June 1920

Michael Silvestri

The Connaught Rangers enjoyed a distinguished history as a British Army regiment from their formation in 1793 until their disbandment in 1922. The Connaughts served the British Empire in places ranging from the Caribbean to Africa to India. Yet, for many Irish people, the Connaught Rangers' greatest feat was not the battle honours they won for queen and empire but a protest they staged in India in the summer of 1920.

On 28 June 1920, a company of the Connaught Rangers stationed at Jullundur on the plains of the Punjab refused to perform their military duties as a protest against the activities of the British Army in Ireland. On the following day, the mutineers sent two emissaries to a company of Connaught Rangers stationed at Solon, about twenty miles away in the foothills of the Himalayas. The soldiers there took up the protest as well and, like their counterparts at Jullundur, flew the tricolour of Ireland, wore 'Sinn Féin' rosettes on their British Army uniforms and sang rebel songs.

The protests were initially peaceful, but on the evening of 1 July around 30 members of the company at Solon, armed with bayonets, attempted to recapture their rifles from the company magazine. The soldiers on guard opened fire, killing two men and wounding another. The incident effectively brought the mutiny to an end, and the mutineers at both Jullundur and Solon were placed under armed guard. Sixty-one men were convicted for their role in the mutiny. Fourteen were sentenced to death by firing squad, but the only soldier whose capital sentence was carried out was Private James Joseph Daly. His life epitomises many prominent features of Irish imperial service. Daly was born in County Galway and grew up in Tyrrellspass, County Westmeath, in a family with a tradition of service to the British Empire. His father and three elder brothers served in the British Army during the First World War, and the sixteen-year-old James briefly served in the Royal Munster Fusiliers during the war as well. In 1919 Daly enlisted in the Connaught Rangers; he had a reputation among his fellow soldiers of possessing not only a strong and somewhat hotheaded personality but also strong republican sympathies. Daly was considered the leader of the mutiny at Solon and the man responsible

26. Members of the 1st battalion of the Connaught Rangers in India. James
Daly is bottom right. (King House Museum, Boyle)

for the failed attack on the magazine. On the morning of 2 November 1920 he
was executed in Dagshai prison in northern India. In a final letter to his mother
the night before his execution, he wrote that 'it is all for Ireland and I am not
afraid to die'; but he also stated that 'I wish to the Lord that I had not started on
getting into this trouble at all'.

With the exception of one man (who died in prison at Dagshai), by the
middle of the following year all of the convicted mutineers had been transferred
to prisons in England to serve out the remainder of their sentences. The
Connaught Rangers, along with three other Irish regiments, were disbanded in
June 1922. Following negotiations between the Irish Free State and the British
government, the mutineers were released from prison and returned to Ireland
early in 1923. Some enlisted in the National Army, others joined the Garda;
many struggled to make a life in post-independence Ireland. Although the
mutineers in many cases received rapturous welcomes in their home town, they
quickly vanished from the public eye.

Yet the Connaught Rangers' mutiny continued to resonate in twentieth-
century Ireland. It has been the subject of books, radio and television
programmes, plays and ballads, and the mutineers have been commemorated
as Irish republican heroes. Historical memories of the 1920 mutiny not only
illuminate the politics of commemoration in independent Ireland but also Irish
imperial and anti-imperial relationships with India.

Indo–Irish nationalist solidarity was well developed by the time of the Connaught Rangers mutiny. In February 1920, four months prior to the mutiny, Éamon de Valera spoke to a packed house of hundreds of Irish and Indian nationalist supporters in New York City. 'Patriots of India,' de Valera declared, 'your cause is identical to ours.' A few weeks earlier, in San Francisco, he had been presented with an Irish tricolour and a ceremonial Sikh sword by representatives of the Indian Gadhar [revolutionary] party. In spite of this anti-imperial affinity, however, the Connaught Rangers made no effort to forge a common cause with Indian nationalists. Indeed, as soldiers of the British Empire, they feared not only retaliation from the British Army but also the prospect of a 'native' revolt if news of their protest leaked out to the surrounding population of the Punjab.

With regard to the 'mutiny' itself, many Indian nationalists nonetheless interpreted the mutiny as a gesture of anti-imperial solidarity. The *Fateh* newspaper of Delhi praised the Jullundur mutineers' actions as an adoption of Mahatma Gandhi's principles of civil disobedience and an illustration of 'how patriotic people can preserve their honour, defy the orders of the Government, and defeat its unjust aims'. In November 1920 the *Independent Hindustan*, a publication of the Gadhar Party in North America, featured an editorial praising the mutineers for their expression of 'sympathy with the gallant Sinn Féiners who are sacrificing their lives for the cause of the Republic of Ireland'. The magazine also published a short story in which an Irish soldier named Shane O'Neill deserts his regiment, exchanges his British Army uniform for a 'native costume' and becomes a leader of an Indian revolutionary cell. 'What's sauce for the goose is sauce for the gander,' he concludes. 'If freedom is good for Ireland, it ought to be good for India.'

Thus, shortly after the events occurred, a mythology of the Connaught Rangers mutiny began to take shape: the mutiny was presented as an anti-imperial protest, an act of Indo–Irish solidarity. Later, some of the mutineers, particularly those

27. One of several drawings produced by mutineers while prisoners in Dagshai. (National Library of Ireland)

with strong republican convictions, emphasised this aspect of their protest. Stephen Lally, one of the leaders of the Jullundur mutiny and later a member of the IRA, recalled: 'I thought we might as well kill two birds with the one stone, and if we could get the Indian National Movement with us it would mean a great victory not alone for Ireland but India as well . . . we could have officered the Native ranks and in a very short time India would have gained her freedom.'

The commemoration of the Connaught Rangers in Ireland similarly elided some of the more complex elements of the protest. While the mutineers' patriotic motivations are clear, many of the soldiers did not have a well-developed understanding of Irish republicanism until they served prison sentences in England. Even then, a number of them petitioned for their release in order to serve the Irish Free State rather than the republican cause during the Civil War. 'I wish to show my loyalty to the Empire by giving my service to the Free State Army of Ireland,' wrote Thomas Devine, one of the Solon mutineers. Nonetheless, by the 1930s the mutineers had been embraced as republican heroes. The Fianna Fáil government granted them pensions in 1936, and the National Graves Association helped to establish a memorial in the Republican Plot of Dublin's Glasnevin Cemetery. The memorial was unveiled on 26 June 1949, a few months after the establishment of the Irish Republic. Adorned with a harp and Celtic-patterned border, it honoured the members of the Connaught Rangers 'who gave their lives during the mutiny and subsequently for Irish freedom'.

The presence of an honour guard of veterans of the Easter Rising at the 1949 ceremony emphasised the identification between the Connaught Rangers and republican heroes. Increasingly, the commemoration of the mutineers also came to emphasise their sacrifice on behalf of the Irish nation, and in particular the sacrifice of the one soldier who had been executed for his role in the protests: Private James Joseph Daly. Over the following two decades, annual commemorations were held at the cenotaph at Glasnevin Cemetery, not on the anniversary of the outbreak of the mutiny in late June but on the anniversary of Daly's execution in November 1920. The cenotaph itself was also sometimes referred to as the 'James Joseph Daly memorial'.

Daly was clearly a complex and charismatic individual, influenced by both Irish republicanism and a family tradition of British Army service. Yet he was quickly transformed into a stereotypical republican martyr. His statement of regret for his role in the mutiny was often omitted when his final letter to his mother was reproduced, and one year after his execution he was portrayed in a poem in the *Westmeath Examiner* as the 'Martyr of Jallandor'. J.C. Keane of Tyrrellspass wrote that the mutineers' goal—'the dream-light of freedom'— 'shone red through their young leader's blood':

His ashes—alas! he lies sleeping—
Afar o'er the ocean's wild tide;

But his memory green we are keeping
In the old land for which he has died;
And Ireland's true sons and true daughters
A prayer for Jim Daly shall breathe,
Who sleeps by the Ganges' dark waters,
So far from his own loved Westmeath.

By the 1960s, the surviving Connaught Rangers, joined by republican
organisations such as the National Graves Association, called for Daly's final
resting place to be moved from beside 'the Ganges' dark waters' to Ireland.
The return of the bodies of the Irish revolutionaries buried abroad was seen as
a national imperative. As the *Irish Press* put it in 1954, 'A nation possesses in the
graves of its dead an assurance of its own permanence'. The return of several

28. A life-size representation of James Daly praying in his cell the night before
his execution at King's House Museum, Boyle. The display stresses the
concern of the mutineers for their friends and family at home rather than
for an abstract republican ideal. (King House Museum, Boyle)

Irish revolutionaries buried in England, notably Sir Roger Casement, whose remains were re-interred in Glasnevin Cemetery in 1965, further spurred calls for the return of what one newspaper called 'Ireland's Loneliest Martyr' from his grave in Dagshai. When Daly's remains were returned to Ireland in 1970, along with those of the two other Connaught Rangers who had been killed at Solon, his sacrifice became connected with contemporary politics: the 'Troubles' in Northern Ireland.

A crowd of more than 6,000 attended the return of Daly's body to Tyrrellspass in October 1970. The ceremonies, held shortly before the 50th anniversary of his execution, elevated Daly to an equal of the greatest heroes of the republican movement. The Irish flag that draped Daly's coffin had previously lain on the coffin of Terence MacSwiney, the lord mayor of Cork who died on hunger strike in October 1920. In a speech at Daly's graveside, Old IRA representative Thomas Malone identified Daly's sacrifice with the republican goal of a thirty-two-county republic: 'It was in the words of Pearse who said the seeds sown by our martyrs of all generations fructify in the hearts of future generations . . . The purpose for which James Daly died had not yet been achieved and much still remained to be done before the republic of Pearse, Tone, Connolly and James Daly was achieved'. Masked members of the IRA later fired a volley in the presence of members of Daly's family.

Daly's reburial in Ireland helped to stir public interest in the Connaught Rangers mutiny. While some press accounts told a straightforward story of British oppression and Irish heroism, two dramatic treatments of the mutiny attempted to grapple with the ambiguities of the protest. Glyn Jones's *The 88*, which premiered at London's Old Vic Theatre in 1979, conveys considerable sympathy for the mutineers, but also portrays the soldiers as contemptuous of Indian servants. Daly refers to an Indian barber (who in the play brings news of the mutiny to Solon) as 'that poor skinny little black bastard I've kicked up the arse so often my foot hurt', while another soldier complains 'God, he stinks of curry'. *The 88* also attracted criticism from the conservative British press in the midst of the Northern Irish conflict. The *Financial Times* commented in a negative review of the play that 'this hardly seems like the most discreet time to put on a play about Irish disaffection in the British Army, when the British Army is trying to keep the peace, with great hardship and difficulty, in Ireland today'.

John Kavanagh's 1994 play *No Comet Seen* captures to an even greater degree the ambiguous nature of the mutiny. The soldiers in the play express sympathy for Indian nationalism, drawing parallels between the 1919 Amritsar Massacre and British Army attacks on Dublin civilians, but also express their fear of falling victim to an Indian revolt. 'God knows what the Indians will try when word gets out—we could have a full-scale uprising on our hands,' warns Daly. Kavanagh's play also portrays an important reality of the mutiny: not all of the

29. James Daly was born in County Galway and grew up in Tyrrellspass, County
Westmeath, in a family with a tradition of service to the British Empire.
His father and three elder brothers served in the British Army during the First
World War, and the sixteen-year-old James briefly served in the Royal Munster
Fusiliers during the war as well. In 1919 Daly enlisted in the Connaught Rangers;
he had a reputation among his fellow soldiers of possessing not only a strong and
somewhat hot-headed personality but also strong republican sympathies.

Connaught Rangers at Jullundur and Solon were willing to cast their lot in with the mutineers. A soldier named Browne from Boyle, Co. Roscommon, argues that he cannot join the protest 'because this is where I belong—the Army. Like me father and his before him. And me uncles too. It's what we Brownes do, you know. My people come from Boyle, the barracks is there—it does a lot for the town . . . I can't be part of this—I just can't'.

The Connaught Rangers barracks in Boyle that Browne refers to now houses the King House Museum. The galleries in this restored eighteenth-century Ascendancy mansion include an exhibit on the history of 'The Fighting Men from Connaught'. The displays feature artefacts of the Connaught Rangers and chronicle the experiences of the soldiers who fought in the regiment during its 120-year history. It concludes with a room devoted to the mutiny, which features a life-size representation of James Daly praying in his cell the night before his execution. A display stresses the concern of the mutineers for their friends and family at home rather than for an abstract republican ideal: 'Many of those in the ranks of the Connaught Rangers could not reconcile the idea of an army, of which they were a part, being mobilised against their own families and friends'.

The Connaught Rangers mutiny demonstrates how Irish imperial relationships cannot always be neatly characterised as anti- or pro-imperial. Soldiers of the British Empire, they staged a protest against the British Army in Ireland. The mutineers feared falling victim to an Indian uprising in the Punjab, but nonetheless inspired Indian nationalists as well as Irish republicans. Various and sometimes conflicting interpretations of the mutiny over the past ninety years demonstrate Ireland's multifaceted relationship with India, as well as the complexities of commemoration in the Irish republic.

Chapter 9

'Prophet of the oppressed nations': Gabriele D'Annunzio and the Irish Republic, 1919–21

Mark Phelan

Following the First World War, the perceived inadequacies of the peace settlement were a major contributing factor to political turmoil in Italy. Coining the phrase 'mutilated victory', the acclaimed poet, politician and soldier Gabriele D'Annunzio (1863–1938) emerged as the high priest of Italian irredentism. Acting on his grievances, he formed a private army, which in September 1919 annexed the disputed Adriatic port of Fiume on behalf of Italy. In so doing, D'Annunzio hoped to inspire a general purification of Italian politics and society. Yet when the fire ignited at Fiume failed to spread to Italy proper, he and his followers found themselves in an isolated position. In response to this setback, D'Annunzio now declared himself *Commandante* of a rogue statelet—the so-called Regency of Carnaro—that posed as a centre for international revolution.

This development was born from D'Annunzio's conviction that Italy was something of a 'proletarian power' whose destiny was to represent the interests of the young, emerging nations of the post-war era. He therefore portrayed his Fiuman adventure as part of a larger contest between the 'Western plutocracies' and the exploited peoples of the world. D'Annunzian Fiume thus became an attractive destination for a curious mix of political extremists. Of this influx, one man in particular, Giuseppe Giulietti, helped to shape subsequent events. Giulietti was the militant leader of the Italian Maritime Workers' Union. Inspired by events in Fiume, in October 1919 he commandeered an Italian cargo ship called the *Persia*. Laden with military equipment, the *Persia* was *en route* to Vladivostok in Russia, where she was to resupply the White Armies then fighting Lenin and the Bolsheviks. In protest at the war in Russia, Giulietti and a volunteer crew boarded the ship and diverted her north to Fiume instead. Suitably armed, D'Annunzio was now in a position to canvass support for a Fiuman-based parody of the League of Nations. Portentously called the 'League of Fiume', this project was to provide a rallying point for the so-called 'oppressed nations' of the world.

To further these ambitious plans, the Fiume Command sanctioned a number of diplomatic missions. Accordingly, in April 1920 the senior Sinn Féin envoy in

30. Gabriele D'Annunzio (right) emerged from the First World War as Italy's most decorated hero. Following the annexation of Fiume, he earned the sobriquet 'the John the Baptist of Fascism'. He and his followers perfected key elements of what became the Fascist liturgy (the black shirt, Roman salute, demagogic speechifying and choreographed street demonstrations). In addition, Fascist corporatism borrowed heavily, albeit in a perverse way, from the governing principles of the Fiuman regime. These truths notwithstanding, D'Annunzio never fully embraced the Mussolini dictatorship. For his part, the Duce (left) resented D'Annunzio as a potential rival. To prevent a public rift, Mussolini supplied D'Annunzio, who had expensive tastes in art, prostitutes and narcotics, with vast sums of money and other rewards. Even so, their relationship remained an uneasy one. In the 1930s the Mussolini–Hitler alliance, which D'Annunzio abhorred, was a particular cause of tension. (Fondazione Il Vittoriale degli Italiani, Archivio Iconografico)

Rome, Seán T. Ó Ceallaigh, learned that, on the proviso that the Irish Republic signed up to the League of Fiume, D'Annunzio was prepared to provide military assistance to the IRA. Recognising that any public dealings with D'Annunzio could be damaging to Irish interests, this offer presented O Ceallaigh with something of a dilemma. For one thing, the cornerstone of Fiuman foreign policy was opposition to the expansion of Anglo–American influence. Clearly, the Irish voiced no objection to any organisation opposed to Great Britain. Yet even though President Wilson's negative attitude towards Irish independence caused resentment at the time, republicans were not prepared to place themselves in opposition to the United States. Moreover, D'Annunzio himself was a notorious philanderer and anti-clericalist whose fondness for irreverence was well known in Ireland. As such, the Dáil government felt disinclined to ally itself with a sworn enemy of the Catholic Church.

The hard-pressed IRA, on the other hand, desperately wanted to access the Fiuman arsenal. In consequence, O'Kelly decided on a policy of prevarication. Giving no more than 'a non-committal answer' about the League of Fiume, he despatched another Sinn Féin envoy, Dónal Hales, to negotiate with D'Annunzio. A native of Bandon, County Cork, Hales's siblings, Tom, Seán and William, were all leading IRA men. Fully informed about the increasingly severe fighting in Munster, Hales pursued his task with an intensity born of concern for family and friends at home. The rapid demise of the League of Fiume, however, fatally undermined Hales's mission. Because of his ultra-nationalist past, D'Annunzio was unable to convince the international left of his commitment to the cause of anti-imperialism. In addition, the nefarious behaviour of Egyptian revolutionaries, who, anticipating the Irish strategy, made off with a large portion of the *Persia*'s rifles before reneging on verbal commitments made to D'Annunzio, caused serious discontent within the Fiume Command. In consequence, the Fiumans were highly protective of their remaining stockpile. Hoarding the balance, they instead concentrated on fomenting revolt in Yugoslavia while at the same time earnestly planning for a future march on Rome.

Despite this setback, the plot to acquire Italian arms now took a new twist. In the late summer of 1920 Hales made contact with a group of regular Italian Army officers. Angered at British 'duplicity', they advised Hales that captured Austrian equipment, then abounding in Italian arsenals, could easily be shipped to Ireland under the guise of 'scrap metal for some Jew in Amsterdam or Oslo'. Via the Anglo-Italian novelist Annie Vivanti, D'Annunzio soon learned of this encounter. Married to a Sinn Féin activist, Vivanti was then performing important propaganda work on behalf of the Irish Republic. As a respected member of the Italian literati, she moved in the same pre-war social circles as D'Annunzio, with whom she forged a strong personal relationship. Suitably exploited by Ó Ceallaigh, this connection revived the poet-warrior's interest in Irish adventures.

To lend speed to this new enterprise, D'Annunzio encouraged the Irish to coordinate their efforts with Benito Mussolini, who, as leader of the nascent Fascist movement, had access to influential elements within the military. Armed with written instructions from D'Annunzio, Vivanti and Ó Ceallaigh travelled to meet the future dictator in Milan. Already keenly interested in the Irish question, Mussolini enthused about the proposed gunrunning venture. Indeed, in a written reply to D'Annunzio, he promised not only to broker a meeting with the military but also to finance any resulting arms shipment to Ireland. Fulfilling the first part of this commitment, Mussolini helped to arrange a meeting at the War Ministry in Rome. Here, on the morning of 21 November 1920—a fateful date in the calendar of the Anglo–Irish struggle, more commonly known as Bloody Sunday—Hales met with a general and a 'senior civil servant', whom one source suggests was actually the then minister for war and future prime minister of Italy, Ivanoe Bonomi. This clandestine conference was highly successful from an Irish point of view. Only anxious that Hales and the IRA should find their own way of removing the arms from Italy, for a 'nominal fee' the Italians promised to supply 20,000 rifles, 500 machine guns and five million rounds of ammunition. Informed of this outcome, the IRA GHQ initiated plans to land these weapons near Cork Harbour in the spring of 1921.

At the time, the Irish in Italy thought nothing other than that they were dealing with corrupt officials who, resentful of the 'mutilated victory', saw an opportunity to line their pockets by selling untraceable Austrian weapons. Yet historical hindsight suggests that high politics also contributed to this remarkable affair. By the winter of 1920, secret negotiations between Rome and Belgrade towards the first Treaty of Rapallo had reached an advanced stage. Under its provisions, Fiume was to become a demilitarised 'free city' along the lines of Danzig in Poland. Furthermore, should D'Annunzio object, the Italians agreed to apply force to effect his removal. To forestall this scenario, the chief architect of the Rapallo agreement, Ivanoe Bonomi, kept a close counsel with the highly ambitious Mussolini. Notwithstanding his public support for 'the hero' in Fiume, the latter feared a D'Annunzian-led *coup d'état*. Thus Mussolini supported the *rapprochement* with Belgrade and connived with Bonomi to bribe D'Annunzio into leaving Fiume voluntarily. Considered from this angle, the intrigues on behalf of the IRA appear calculated to pander to D'Annunzio's wider interests in advance of Rapallo. If so, it is also probable that Bonomi and Mussolini anticipated that, post-Rapallo, the Irish might provide them with lasting relief from their mutual problem. Given that he was a self-proclaimed 'man of action' with a thirst for adventure and publicity, there was every possibility that a deflated D'Annunzio might join the gunrunning expedition to Ireland, thereby removing himself from Italy altogether.

Subsequent events would appear to support this hypothesis. Unmoved by bribes, D'Annunzio eventually 'declared war' on Italy. Hostilities were

Switzerland

France

South Tyrol
Trento
Trentino
Riza
Milan

Turin

Gulf of
Genoa

Austria-Hungary

Gorizia
Trieste
Istria
Fiume

Pola

Croatia

Florence

Ancona

Zadar

Sebenico

Dalmatia

Bosnia

Serbia

Corsica

Italy

ROME

Adriatic sea

Montenegro

Albania

Sardinia

Naples

Tyrrhenian
Sea

Brindisi

Valona

Gulf of
Taranto

Italy Pre 1914

Territory promised under 1915 Treaty of London

Territory actually ceded to Italy,
1919- '20

Disputed City of Fiume
(ceded to Italy 1924)

Territory occupied by Italy,
1914- '20

Sicily

Ionian Sea

Italy and the
Treaty of London 1915

31. Following the First World War, the perceived inadequacies of the peace settlement were a major contributing factor to political turmoil in Italy. (Tomás Ó Brogáin)

short-lived, however. A bombardment on Christmas Eve 1920, in which D'Annunzio himself suffered an injury, finally brought his burlesque regime to an ignominious end. Nevertheless, having obtained a largely bloodless victory, the authorities in Rome granted a general amnesty to the defeated garrison. D'Annunzio himself remained in Fiume for some weeks to recuperate, from

32. Paris, May 1919—Seán T. Ó Ceallaigh (centre) with Mr and Mrs Charles Gavan Duffy on the way to a meeting with Georges Clemenceau. O'Kelly regularly entertained other disaffected diplomats, including representatives from D'Annunzio's city-state, who had gathered in the French capital. In exchange for weapons, D'Annunzio (inset) subsequently invited O'Kelly to participate in the short-lived 'League of Fiume'. (Military Archives; New York Times Historical Archive)

whence, amidst widespread rumours that he was destined for Ireland or some other troubled part of the British Empire, he retreated to his villa on the shores of Lake Garda.

Meanwhile, the republican leadership had selected a Cork officer with seafaring experience, Cmdt Michael Leahy, to travel to Italy. Travelling incognito as a clerical student bound for Rome, Leahy arrived in Genoa in March 1921. On arrival, he learned that Hales and Giuseppe Giulietti had finalised arrangements for removing the arms from Italy. The Maritime Workers' Union owned a sailing collier named the *Stella Maris*, which was made available for the enterprise. Normally travelling outbound to Newcastle in ballast, on her next voyage Leahy and an Italian crew planned to sail the ship south to Rome, where she was to take aboard her military cargo. At this point it appears that the only issue preventing the scheme from reaching a successful conclusion was money. By now, the mooted 'nominal fee' had been set at the princely sum of £10,000. Mussolini, moreover, had evidently reneged on his previous assurances, and the cost involved gave Dublin serious pause for thought. Nevertheless, indicating that funds would be forthcoming, Dáil Minister for Finance Michael Collins instructed Hales to bide his time until a suitable means of transferring the money to Genoa was found.

With the initiative stalled, Hales and Leahy embarked upon an impromptu tour of northern Italy. Travelling in the company of D'Annunzio's confidants, they first travelled to Milan, where they met with Vivanti and leading Fascists. From there the party travelled onwards to Lake Garda, where D'Annunzio himself entertained them. According to Leahy, D'Annunzio's men pleaded to be allowed to travel aboard the *Stella Maris*. In so doing, they revived plans, first mooted in the spring of 1920, to send an expeditionary force to Ireland to fight alongside the IRA. Meanwhile, the records of the Dáil Ministry for Foreign Affairs suggest that D'Annunzio himself was agreeable to reappearing in Ireland as the fêted benefactor of the Republic. According to another senior Sinn Féin diplomat, George Gavan Duffy, the former *Commandante* felt 'bitterly disappointed at the king [of Italy] for firing him out of Fiume' and wanted 'a new field, and thinks of Ireland, India and Egypt'. Clearly excited

33. *Il Popolo d'Italia*, 29 August 1920—in his capacity as editor of the Fascist daily newspaper, Benito Mussolini invested heavily in the Irish question. Courtesy of Irish activists in Italy, he had ready access to republican propaganda. Mussolini's editorials, which eulogised Sinn Féin at the expense of the British, complemented these reports. Yet these pronouncements were rhetorical and tactical rather than genuine. Reflecting the catch-all intent of early fascism, they appealed simultaneously to Italian anti-imperialists and nationalists who believed that Britain had abandoned Italy at the Paris peace conference. As demonstrated here, grandiose statements on international affairs also sought to create the impression that Mussolini was somehow a 'statesman in waiting'. In this example he offers an opinion on Terence McSwiney's hunger strike, Arab revolts in Italian-occupied Libya, the Soviet–Polish War, and the likelihood of a future rapprochement between Russia and Germany.

34. Fiume, spring 1920—D'Annunzio surrounded by his followers, some of whom volunteered to fight alongside the IRA. Encouraged by their leader, these self-styled 'legionaries' lived a life of excess while in Fiume; even so, they were capable soldiers, for many had served with the Arditi, élite troops of the Italian Army. (Fondazione Il Vittoriale degli Italiani, Archivio Iconografico)

by the prospect, Gavan Duffy wanted to secure the issue in Ireland's favour by approaching D'Annunzio with a written invitation from the Dáil.

Unfortunately for D'Annunzio and Gavan Duffy—and one must suspect for Mussolini and the Italian government also—this suggestion was not taken up by a cautious President de Valera. Revealing that he harboured unconventional plans of his own about how best to subvert the British Empire, de Valera instead invited D'Annunzio to try his luck in Soviet Moscow, and from there to march on an unsuspecting India!

Tempting though it is to speculate on the matter, the historical record does not reveal whether D'Annunzio felt revitalised or further humbled by de Valera's fantastic suggestion. Either way, the gunrunning plot collapsed in April 1921. Upon learning that the Royal Navy was keeping a watchful eye out for the *Stella Maris*, Michael Collins aborted the mission. Exactly how the British uncovered the plot remains something of a mystery. Regardless, in the interests of protecting his own intelligence-gathering operations, Collins instructed Hales to remain tight-lipped about why the Irish had abandoned the enterprise. Hales rigidly observed this instruction until his deposition to the

Bureau of Military History in 1953. Thus rumours and innuendo, including tales of cabinet-level treachery, about the failure to procure Italian weapons abounded within the Munster IRA for years to come.

The ultimate failure of the enterprise notwithstanding, it remains an interesting footnote in the history of the Anglo–Irish conflict. Attempting to exploit the radical plans of D'Annunzian Fiume, the IRA discovered unlikely patrons in the form of Benito Mussolini and the Italian military. Not alone did this affair demonstrate an unusual interconnectivity between the post-war strife in Ireland and Italy, it also, perhaps, rendered anachronistic a legendary Mussolini boast. When discussing a recently deceased D'Annunzio in 1938, Mussolini allegedly claimed that, 'When you have a rotten tooth you have two possibilities open to you: either you pull the tooth or you fill it with gold. With D'Annunzio it was always easier to fill him with gold.' If credible, these remarks, while neatly summarising the difficult relationship between Mussolini and D'Annunzio after the Fascist seizure of power, are not a complete résumé of their dealings. Rather, the evidence suggests that, during the autumn and winter of 1920–21, Mussolini and the faltering Italian regime tried to find a cheaper and more effective way of extracting the troublesome tooth that was Gabriele D'Annunzio by foisting him upon the Irish republic.

Chapter 10

Bloody Sunday, 1920: the military inquiry

Tim Carey and Marcus de Búrca

The events of 'Bloody Sunday', 21 November 1920, are generally regarded as having marked a decisive turning point in the military struggle between the British forces and the IRA. Three separate but connected events occurred on Bloody Sunday. First came the killings by Michael Collins' 'Squad' of twelve alleged British intelligence agents in their Dublin residences that morning; two auxiliary policemen were also killed. In the afternoon came the killing by British forces of fourteen civilians—including a Gaelic footballer, Michael Hogan, who was playing for Tipperary that day—at Croke Park in what was assumed to have been a direct reprisal. Finally, in the evening came the arrest and killing (in somewhat murky circumstances) of two high-ranking Dublin IRA officers, Brigadier Dick McKee and Vice Brigadier Peadar Clancy. In all, over thirty people died within fifteen hours on that fateful day in Dublin.

The assassinations of the British officers virtually crippled the intelligence operations of Dublin Castle. Bloody Sunday also marked an emotional turning point in the War of Independence and has gone down as a central event in nationalist history. Although thousands were in attendance that day the exact events which led to the killings have never been conclusively proven with each side contradicting the other. The only public statement issued by the authorities was one hurriedly drafted by Dublin Castle. It blamed the IRA for shooting at Crown forces when they arrived to raid Croke Park. No authoritative account from the British side had ever been published. But the eventual release around the turn of the century of the official British record of a military inquiry, known to have been carried out in lieu of an inquest on the fourteen Irish fatalities but held in camera, finally enabled rival accounts to be compared.

The file in question is retained in the National Archives of the United Kingdom at Kew, and contains the proceedings of the military inquiry held at some time before 8 December 1920, and probably at military headquarters, Parkgate, Dublin. The documents released contain no date or precise location. The inquiry was held in camera under the Restoration of Order in Ireland Act (effectively a successor to the wartime Defence of the Realm Act). The personnel of the three-man inquiry were Major R. Bunbury, president, with Lieutenant S. H. Winterbottom of the 1st Lancashire Fusiliers and Lieutenant B. J. Key

35. A picture alleged to depict the so-called 'Cairo Gang' the nickname referred to either previous service in the middle east, or the Cairo Cafe on Dublin's Grafton St – some of them were among the twelve British intelligence officers assassinated by Michael Collins's 'squad' on the morning of 21 November 1920. (Hulton Getty Picture Collection, London)

of the 2nd Worcester Regiment as members. There are two different versions of the proceedings; one is handwritten and the other typed; the contents are practically identical. Evidence was given by over thirty witnesses—depending on which set of documents one relies. The details of the identities of the witnesses were generally withheld although they were mainly from the RIC and Auxiliaries. In the case of a handful of DMP witnesses, one has no problem in identifying the force to which they belonged. Uncharacteristically, one was even named and his rank specified.

In addition to the main inquiry there was also a separate one, again 'in lieu of an inquest' (under the Restoration of Order in Ireland Act) into the deaths of fourteen civilians at Croke Park—John Scott, James Matthews, Jeremiah O'Leary, Patrick O'Dowd, Jane Boyle, William Robinson, Thomas Hogan, James Burke, Michael Feery, James Teehan, Joseph Traynor, Thomas Ryan, Michael Hogan and Daniel Carroll. In all these cases evidence was given by relatives who had identified the bodies and by doctors who had received and examined them in Dublin hospitals. Documents relating to the inquiry showed that the verdicts of this second inquiry were, predictably, death in most of the cases from bullet wounds, with heart failure listed as the cause of death in the remaining cases. The descriptions make grim reading. In the inquest on the death of Thomas Hogan, Dr Patrick Moran, of the Mater Hospital, stated:

> Thomas Hogan was admitted to this hospital at 4 pm on November 21st. There was a small round wound 3/8 inch in diameter under the spine of the right scapula. There was a large round wound one inch in diameter just beneath the acromion process in front. This was apparently an exit wound. There were two other small wounds a quarter inch in diameter one inch above acromion process, and about an inch apart. These might have been caused by bone splinters. On admission the patient was bleeding profusely, and was in a state of severe collapse. The right arm was amputated on Monday, 22nd November. The shoulder joint was found to be completely disorganised. The head of the humerus was completely severed from the shaft and about 2 inches of the shaft was shattered. The auxiliary border of the scapula was also shattered. A small piece of nickel casing was found in the region of the shoulder joint. Gas gangrene set in after the operation and the patient died at 12.30 on November 26th. Death was in my opinion due to toxaemia following gas gangrene following gunshot wounds.

There are undoubtedly difficulties taking on board such material. Because the sittings of the main inquiry were held in camera, no witness had any legal representation and there appears to have been no cross-examination. There was only one exception to this routine. After five military witnesses and three ambulance men had been heard, i.e. between witnesses 8 and 9, two lawyers briefly addressed the court. James Comyn BL said he was led by Michael Comyn KC (his brother), that they appeared for the family of Jane Boyle (a twenty-six-year-old woman killed at Croke Park) and wished to produce witnesses. However, Michael Comyn KC told the court that because the inquiry was 'held behind closed doors' he would not take part in the inquiry, and led his party out.

On 8 December 1920 the verdict of the court of inquiry was issued. It found that during a raid on Croke Park on 21 November 1920 by a mixed force of RIC, auxiliary police and military, firing was started by unknown civilians, either as a warning of the raid or else to create a panic, that the injuries to dead civilians were inflicted by rifle or revolver fire by the RIC from the bridge over the Royal Canal, some of whom fired over the crowd's heads, others of whom fired into the crowd at persons believed to be trying to evade arrest. It also found that the RIC firing was done without orders and in excess of what was required, but that no firing came from the auxiliary police or the military, except that soldiers in an armoured car (at the St James's Avenue exit) fired a burst of fire into the air to stop the crowd from breaking through and out of the ground.

Appended to the inquiry report is a copy (marked 'Secret and V. Urgent!') dated 21 November 1920 of the (unsigned) order given by a brigade major, Infantry Brigade, to the RIC and containing details of the operation planned to take place that day at Croke Park. The ground was to be surrounded and pickets placed at specified points, e.g. on the railway and at the three known exits. One infantry platoon was to be kept in reserve and at 3.15 pm two (army) armoured cars would meet the mixed RIC and auxiliary police at Fitzroy Avenue (opposite the main entrance). A quarter-hour before the end of the match a special intelligence officer would warn the crowd by megaphone that anybody trying to leave other than by the exits would be shot, and that all males would be stopped and searched.

The opinion of the competent military authority (dated 11 December 1920), which convened the court of inquiry, was:

 (i)   that it agreed with the court findings [summarised above];
 (ii) that the first shots were fired by the crowd and led to the panic; &
 (iii) that the firing on the crowd was carried out without orders and was indiscriminate and unjustifiable, with the exception of any shooting which took place inside the enclosure.

This opinion was signed by Major-General G. F. Boyd, commanding officer, Dublin.

Because much of the evidence at the court of inquiry is at variance with accounts given by Irish survivors (including at least two of the thirty footballers involved), the credibility of this inquiry, published so long after all involved on both sides are dead, must be open to challenge. However, the withholding, not only of the identities of witnesses (all also presumably dead), but also of the identities of the forces (other than the DMP) to which they belonged, present difficulties to any challenge nearly a century years after the event. Nevertheless the inquiry cannot be discounted as it offers the only known piece of official documentation to one of the most well-known events in modern Irish history.

The central point in dispute was: who fired first? Common to all reports is that the firing started at the south-west corner of the ground (that is, the corner where Jones's Road crosses the Royal Canal). Was the government claim that their forces were fired on first true? There were undoubtedly IRA men in the grounds that day. At the time there was certainly overlap between membership of the IRA and membership of the GAA. It is certainly not out of the question that shots could have been fired at the Crown forces. If that was the case, it was obviously an extremely irresponsible act.

36. Neil Jordan's depiction in *Michael Collins* of British armoured cars bursting through the main gate of Croke Park and firing their machine guns on the crowd was criticised as pure invention. In fact armoured cars were involved but outside the ground and, according to the enquiry, the one at the St James's Avenue exit fired fifty rounds. (Warner Brothers)

The alternative theory is that the RIC and Auxiliaries raided Croke Park in reprisal for the attacks that morning. Such reprisals were becoming common. Balbriggan had been sacked in September. Less than three weeks after Bloody Sunday Cork city felt the brunt of such a reprisal. These were mainly unofficial, but little was done on the part of high-ranking officers to dissuade their men, who felt justified in exacting revenge on a population protecting what they regarded as a 'murder gang'.

The inquiry was by no means conclusive but it does shed some light on a number of points. Several of the RIC witnesses contend that the firing began from inside the ground, presumably by armed spectators, before any Crown forces had entered. Admittedly, down the years this allegation has occasionally been made. But precisely how this allegation, even if true, justified the shooting dead of at least fourteen unarmed civilians (including two young boys and a twenty-six-year-old woman), as well as the wounding of scores of spectators, by the mixed force of police and military, is not explained in the inquiry's conclusions. Indeed, the court of inquiry found the shootings to be unauthorised and far in excess of what was deemed appropriate even if the Crown forces were fired on first. The documents also reveal that a total

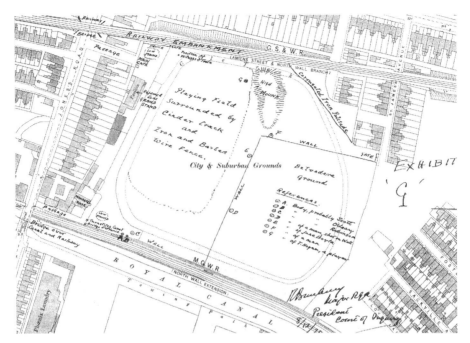

37. Detail of 'exhibit "g"', the map used by the enquiry, and signed (bottom right-hand corner) by its president, Major R. Bunbury. (Public Record Office, London)

of 228 rounds of small arms ammunition were fired by the RIC (including Auxiliaries) and that the army machine-gun at the St James's Avenue exit fired a total of fifty rounds.

Of those who admitted to firing rounds one member of the Crown forces was especially graphic:

On November 21st 1920 I was in the second lorry of the convoy to Croke Park. The lorry halted just over the canal bridge. I saw no civilians on the bridge. There were some civilians in the passage leading to the turnstiles. I got out and went to the turnstiles as quickly as I could. As I got to the turnstiles I heard shots. I am certain they were revolver shots, a few shots fired quickly. They were fired inside the field. I tried to get through the turnstiles and found that they were locked. When getting over them a bullet hit the wall convenient to my head. This was the wall on the right hand side inside the archway and splinters of brick and mortar hit me in the face. It could not have been fired from outside the field. As I got inside I landed on my hands and feet. I saw young men aged between 20 and 25 running stooping among the crowd, away from me between the fence and the wall. I pursued and discharged my revolver in their direction.

My duties were identification of persons. I was in plain clothes having a Glengarry cap in my pocket for identification by my own men if necessary. Having been fired at I used my own discretion in returning fire. I aimed at individual young men who were running away trying to conceal themselves in the crowd. I used a .450 revolver and service ammunition. I chased them across the ground nearly to the wall on the east side. I then saw that a number of people were going back towards the main gate by which I came in. I rushed to that gate and took up my position outside to try and carry out my duties of identification. I stayed there until the ground was cleared, that is about an hour and a half.

Many of the RIC witnesses stated that when the first of their members got out of their lorry a group of civilians, ranging in number from 3-4 to 8-9, who were at the start of the passage from the canal bridge down to the canal entry turnstiles and who appeared to be acting in concert, turned and ran at speed through the turnstiles. Some of the party, it was alleged, fired back in the direction of the men dismounting from the lorry. It is this alleged engagement between armed IRA men and the raiding party that is at the core of apportioning blame for the deaths at Croke Park.

38. Tipperary footballer Michael Hogan (after whom the stand was later named)— the only player killed on Bloody Sunday. Ironically, Hogan was a member of the IRA in his native Tipperary. (GAA Museum)

Among those backing up this version of events was the eighth witness who stated:

> On 21st November I was in the first car of the convoy detailed to go to Croke Park. Immediately we came to the canal bridge on the rise overlooking the park. I observed several men rushing back from the top of the bridge towards the entrance gate of the park. I observed three of them turning backward as they ran and discharging revolvers in our direction. Almost immediately the firing appeared to be taken up by members of the crowd inside the enclosure. At this time the members of our party were jumping out of the cars. Most of them rushed down the incline towards the entrance gate.

The first and second DMP witnesses were on Jones' Road near the canal bridge. Neither reported seeing any civilians who could have threatened the Crown forces, nor did they report any shots being fired outside the ground. The first DMP constable called stated that shortly after 3.30 pm about fifteen lorries of military and RIC arrived at the canal bridge entrance. The occupants of the first car ran down the passage leading to the football grounds. He stated that he did not know who started the firing but he reported that a military officer came running up to the bridge and said 'what is all the firing about, stop that firing'.

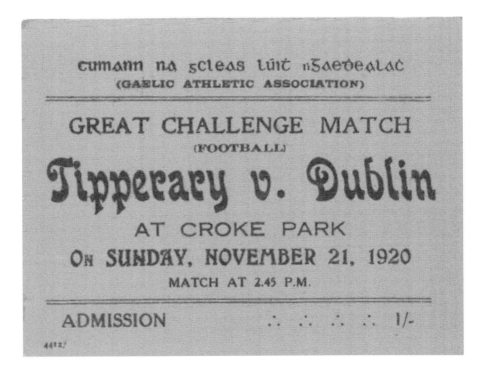

View of the Magnificent Stadium at Croke Park, Dublin, showing portion of the Extensive Stands. Athletic and Cycling Events, as well as Camogie, Hurling and Football Competitions will take place here for the Tailteann Games

40. Croke Park in 1924, showing the 'cinder track and iron and barbed wire fence' referred to on the map. The 'main gate' (off picture) was to the right of the taller stand ('pavilion' or 'grandstand' on the map). The long low stand did not exist in 1920. The canal end passage and turnstile, where the firing started, is to its left. (GAA Museum)

The third DMP officer was on duty further down Jones' Road, outside the main entrance to Croke Park. He gave evidence concerning a separate group of RIC who arrived at the main gate:

On Sunday 21st inst. I was on duty outside the main entrance to Croke Park in Jones's Road. At about 3.25 p.m. I saw six or seven large lorries accompanied by two armoured cars, one in front and one behind, pass along the Clonliffe Road from Drumcondra towards Ballybough. Immediately after a small armoured car came across Jones's Road from Fitzroy Avenue and pulled up at the entrance of the main gate. Immediately after that, three small Crossley lorries pulled up in Jones's Road. There were about ten or twelve men dressed in RIC uniforms in each. When they got out of the cars they started firing in the air which I thought was blank ammunition, and almost immediately firing started all round the ground.

On the face of it the DMP evidence differs from other Crown forces witnesses on the crucial question of who fired first. Since they might be expected to corroborate the evidence of other forces their testimony may be the most significant of all that given to the inquiry.

The evidence of two of three spectators who gave evidence to the inquiry, one of whom is easily identified (see below), is of interest, since it too is in conflict with the bulk of the evidence from the RIC, Auxiliaries and military. Witness 9, who appears to have accompanied to the game Jeremiah O'Leary (killed) stated that the first shooting came from the canal bridge, and that it came from Auxiliaries ('men in RIC caps and khaki trousers'). According to this witness, the officer in charge at the bridge (probably from the first lorry to reach the bridge) also wore this uniform and had a bonnet, i.e. a Glengarry cap, peculiar to the 'Auxies'.

The next witness (number 10) described himself as manager of Croke Park. Although also unnamed this was Luke O'Toole, general secretary of the GAA, who resided beside the canal bridge. He told of how, from a low mound, then on the site of the recently demolished Nally Stand (to which he had moved from a seat in the stand when firing began), he saw firing commence at the canal end. Of all the statements known to have been made after Bloody Sunday, this is believed to be the only one made by a GAA official to the British authorities. However, O'Toole died suddenly in 1929 long before any statements from the Irish side were ever made, either to Irish newspapers or to the Bureau of Military History. The shootings at Croke Park lasted only a matter of minutes. Yet almost a century later the events of that day are still emotive and controversial. The overall findings of the military inquiry, as released, must be viewed with some suspicion, but nonetheless cast a great deal of light on this critical event.

Chapter 11

The burning of Cork, 1920: the fire
service response

Pat Poland

In the long period of turmoil from late 1920 to the spring of 1923, Cork City would be buffeted by acts of shocking violence, not least among them the burning of the main shopping district by Crown forces in December 1920.

If quirky monikers were being handed out, the city during that unhappy period might have qualified as the 'arson capital of Europe'. Early in April 1920 Michael Collins ordered the launch of a concentrated series of arson attacks on hundreds of abandoned police barracks with a view to preventing them from being reoccupied. Simultaneously, over 100 Revenue offices were targeted, including those on Cork's South Mall and South Terrace. Even as the city-centre fires raged, a further thirteen RIC stations in the suburbs and county were destroyed. Throughout July, several more were burned down, with the

41. Fire chief Capt. Alfred J. Hutson (back row, left) and members of Cork Fire
    Brigade c. 1920.

fire brigade being prevented by armed young men from getting to work, or, on occasion, being stopped by force of arms from leaving the three city fire stations. The IRA's objective was to make it impossible, ultimately, for the British administration to function in Ireland.

During October notices began appearing in the press and on flyers around the city, purporting to be from a shadowy body styling itself the 'Anti-Sinn Féin Society'. Similar notices were signed 'Black and Tans' and 'Secretary of Death or Victory League'. All warned of dire consequences if attacks on Crown forces and members of the loyalist community did not cease forthwith. Their appearance heralded a serious escalation in the workload of Cork Fire Brigade, headed up by the veteran Captain Alfred J. Hutson (who was in fact English). In 1920 the Cork Fire and Ambulance Brigade had been in existence for forty-three years, having been established as a municipal entity in 1877, and had been commanded by Hutson since 1891. Operating out of the Central Fire Station on Sullivan's Quay (on the south channel of the River Lee), and substations at Grattan Street (city centre) and Shandon Street (northern suburbs), it comprised ten full-time men and thirteen part-time auxiliaries. The latter were, typically, employed in the city engineer's department of Cork Corporation; after their normal day's work, they performed a raft of non-fire-fighting duties, such as watchroom duty, theatre duty, etc., and responded to fires on the 'second alarm'. Unlike the major conurbations of Dublin and Belfast, however, Cork lagged behind in the matter of modern fire-fighting technology, having, for example, no motor pumps. Instead, it relied on horse-drawn hose-reels that tapped directly into the city's water mains when tackling fires. An ageing Merryweather steam pump was pressed into action as the occasion demanded.

Beginning with the attempted burning of the City Hall on 9 October, during the following weeks the brigade would be tasked with over twenty serious incidents, all related to the independence struggle and many involving the destruction of premises used by Sinn Féin for cultural activities. Throughout 1920 Cork city and county lurched from crisis to crisis, in a rising crescendo of violence. The killing of policemen and members of the Crown forces was invariably followed by reprisals, with members of the independence movement being targeted and shot.

On 28 November 1920 at Kilmichael in County Cork, seventeen members of the Auxiliary Division were killed and one seriously wounded by an IRA flying column under Tom Barry. Three Volunteers also died in the encounter. Less than two weeks later, on 11 December, their city counterparts launched an ambush on an Auxiliary patrol at Dillon's Cross in Cork's northern suburbs, just a few hundred metres from the main garrison at Victoria (now Collins) Barracks. One auxiliary policeman died and eleven were wounded.

Sporadic guerrilla activity against forces such as the Black and Tans and Auxiliaries achieved only a limited military impact, sometimes at high cost to the general, non-belligerent population. Ever since the Kilmichael ambush, a palpable air of trepidation had hung over Cork City. Now, following the Dillon's Cross ambush, the fire brigade was alerted to a number of houses blazing nearby, torched as an official reprisal 'for failure to give warning of an ambush against the police'. Fire Brigade Headquarters transferred the call to the Grattan Street station, which responded under Senior Fireman Timothy Ring. The route they travelled took them through St Patrick's Street in the city centre, and as they turned into the thoroughfare pandemonium reigned. Alexander Grant and Co., a major up-market department store, which stretched from St Patrick's Street back to Grand Parade, was blazing, the fire being fuelled by drunken Auxiliaries intent on creating havoc. In view of the seriousness of the fire, with its potential to flare into a conflagration, Ring decided to go at once to the Central Fire Station to apprise Hutson of the situation.

As the men quickly prepared the horses and equipment, the ever-methodical Hutson had a number of tasks to perform. First, he rang the military at Victoria Barracks and requested them, in view of the enormity of the task facing him in the city centre, to take their fire-fighting appliances to Dillon's Cross. He later deposed that 'they took no notice of my request'. Then he rang the duty

42. The only known photograph of the burning of Cork, taken during the night of 11/12 December 1920. For those watching from the suburbs, outside the curfew zone, the whole skyline was a shifting orange glow. (*The American Commission on Conditions in Ireland: Interim Report* [1921])

engineer at Cork waterworks to ascertain the situation there. Had there been any interference from the auxiliary police or any other quarter? He breathed a sigh of relief when the answer was in the negative. Finally, he looked at his watch. Low tide, he recalled, was at twenty-two minutes past midnight. Faced with an ebbing tide, he could not depend on the steam fire engine to pump water from the river, but, if required, would have it in place to take full advantage of high water at 6.25 in the morning. It was the period of the new moon, when the tides have the greatest range and strength, and the spring tides would mean that the low tides were very low and the high tides were very high.

Hutson knew that the combined capacity of the two city water reservoirs was some four million gallons, supplied by pumping plant including three triple extension engines and a set of water-powered turbines. The ordinary requirements of the population, including industry, were up to four million gallons a day, however, which would mean, in the normal course of events, that if the reservoirs were not replenished both tanks would be empty in just twenty-four hours. When the great amount of water required for the fire-fighting task was factored in, the fire chief could face the ultimate doomsday scenario of having a city on fire with no water available in the mains to fight it (to say nothing of the havoc that the lack of water would have wreaked amongst the general population). This is why it was important for Hutson to know that it (probably) had not occurred to the Auxiliaries to disable the pumping station; if it had, the consequences would surely have been devastating The failure to exploit this weak link in the city's fire defences gave Cork a chance.

For all the firemen knew, a fusillade of bullets might greet them upon arriving in St Patrick's Street. Firefighters are used to taking control at an incident, containing the damage, minimising injuries as far as possible, and setting its boundaries. This one, however, was on a scale beyond their collective experience. Multiplying and mutating rapidly, it was unlike anything any of them, including their London-trained and experienced chief, had ever encountered. The brigade was now dealing with the dreaded conflagration, a fire involving a number of buildings. For such a task it was singularly under-equipped, and Hutson had to make the unpalatable decision to 'triage': many premises would simply have to be allowed to burn while he did his best to contain the fires within a specified area. As the enormous fires sucked in more and more oxygen to feed their insatiable demands, the paintwork on the opposite side of the wide St Patrick's Street began to blister. Upon seeing this, the fire chief must have been at his most apprehensive throughout that long night. By 11 pm most of the south side of St Patrick's Street was on fire. The columns of flame now moved further southwards, feeding greedily on the buildings in Morgan Street, Robert Street, Oliver Plunkett Street (north side), Cook Street, Winthrop Street, Winthrop Lane, Caroline Street, Maylor Street and Merchant's Street. Twenty of the principal establishments with a footprint on St Patrick's Street were involved,

43. Cork (left) and Dublin fire-engines pumping water from the River Lee at
    Merchant's Quay. (NLI)

as well as a further thirty businesses on the side-streets. The total area now on
fire was some five acres—an area about the size of three football pitches. For
those watching from the suburbs, outside the curfew zone, the whole skyline
was a shifting orange glow. Elsewhere across the city, on Grand Parade, Oliver
Plunkett Street, Washington Street and Bridge Street, business premises were
looted and sacked by Auxiliaries and Black and Tans. The City Hall, municipal
offices and the nearby Carnegie Free Library were bombed and set on fire, the
party of firemen sent to guard them being shot at and Mills bombs lobbed in
their direction.

By Sunday afternoon (12 December) the Cork fire-fighters were all but
worn out. On duty for well over thirty hours without respite (their duty
shift began at 7am on Saturday morning) and with the outcome still far from
certain (who knew but that there would be further incendiarism that night),
the decision was made to request reinforcements from the nearest available fire
brigades. Lord Mayor O'Callaghan telegraphed his counterparts in Limerick
(sixty-three miles distant) and Dublin (163 miles) and the replies were swift and
positive: help would soon be on the way. Members of Limerick Fire Brigade
arrived by private car, laden down with fire gear, while Dublin dispatched
its latest Leyland motor fire-engine with a crew under their chief officer,
John Myers. The Dublin contingent travelled on a specially commissioned

Above and below: 44. The morning after—Cork citizens pick their way through the rubble.

train from Kingsbridge (now Heuston) Station, accompanied by a large press contingent. Each of the outside brigades performed sterling service, remaining in Cork until the following Wednesday.

Throughout the night, firemen were harassed, intimidated and shot at by Crown forces. It was nothing short of a miracle that all missed vital organs, but four firemen had to be taken to hospital for treatment of bullet wounds. The brigade member working the Merryweather steam pump from the river suffered a shattered nose (while unbelievably, there were no fatalities directly resulting from the fires, in the early hours of Sunday morning brothers Cornelius and Jeremiah Delany, along with their brother-in-law, were shot by police in their home, both brothers succumbing to their wounds). The city streets were awash with precious water flowing uselessly from hoses that had been ripped open by bayonets. The military deliberately drove their lorries over the hoses until they burst. But not all Crown forces behaved badly; some actually helped the firemen to man the hoses, and one (perhaps a Black and Tan) saved the unconscious senior fireman, Ring (later, in 1928, chief officer), from a burning building. And a night not renowned for its levity did not pass without its moments of incongruous farce. Eighteen-year-old auxiliary fireman Michael Murphy, in a 1960 radio interview, recalled:

A Black and Tan jumped up on top of me. "Come on", he says, "we'll have a waltz", and I put down the hose and I was waltzing with him. I noticed, him being a small man, he had a rifle … which protruded up under my chin. I said to him, "Here, boss, look at where that's protruding, it's rather dangerous". He had a bottle in his pocket and I was afraid the trigger was hitting the bottle, and he said to me, "I'm Sunny Jim, and I never fired a shot in Cork!", and with that he caught his rifle and threw it into the middle of Patrick's Street.

General Strickland's report on the burnings (deposited in the UK National Archives at Kew and released in 1999) was suppressed by Prime Minister Lloyd George, as it portrayed aspects of the British campaign in Ireland in a very bad light. In so doing, he failed to recognize, it would seem, that nothing inflates rumour as swiftly as concealment. Although not published, this did not stop others who were privy to its contents from commenting on it. General Sir Nevil Macready, the last General Officer Commanding British forces in Ireland, in his 1924 autobiography *Annals of an Active Life* wrote 'there was no doubt that the fires and subsequent looting were the work of a company of the Auxiliary Division'.

Cork Corporation did not engage with the official inquiry held in Victoria Barracks as they insisted that an impartial body should conduct the investigation. When this was denied, they resolved to take no part in the proceedings, directing their officials, including Capt. Hutson and the fire brigade staff, to do likewise.

45. Hutson on his appointment in 1891.

Just like soldiers going into battle, all fire brigade operations depend on an element of luck for their successful conclusion. From the moment Alfred Hutson and his men turned out luck was on their side, even though they were not then aware of it. If the Crown forces had been better co-ordinated, more imaginative, and not befuddled by alcohol—above all else, if they had turned their attention to the other side of St Patrick's Street as well or disabled the City Waterworks—who can say what the night's outcome might have been? Instead of a burnt area of five acres, Cork could have suffered a far worse fate.

Chapter 12

The War of Independence in the northern counties

Pierse Lawlor

For the people of Ulster the events taking place in the rest of Ireland during 1918–19 seemed remote. As IRA attacks on the RIC gathered pace, however, the ripples of the violence spread northwards and by 1920 the war was on the doorstep of the nationalist and unionist populations in Ulster.

The War of Independence in the northern counties had an additional dimension to that in the rest of the island. Unionists had armed themselves in 1913 as the Ulster Volunteer Force (UVF) to resist Home Rule 'by all means', and by 1920 had reorganised to combat increasing attacks by the IRA. UVF units were later incorporated en masse into the Ulster Special Constabulary when it was set up in October 1920. There was also a latent sectarianism, which bubbled to the surface each year during the Orange 'marching season', and this had a significant impact in raising tensions, as religious animosity was added to the mix. It was inevitable that there would be a sectarian element to the conflict in the northern counties.

This is an aspect of the War of Independence that both sides sought to play down but of which both were guilty to a greater or lesser extent. It is clear that the IRA did not set out with a sectarian agenda. Their focus was on attacking the Crown forces and it mattered little whether those being attacked or killed were Catholic or Protestant. As the conflict went on, however, they were drawn into sectarian killings, particularly in Belfast. For many of the loyalist population the distinction between nationalist, Catholic, Sinn Féin supporter and IRA activist was not just blurred but non-existent. Unionist leaders had, after all, for years impressed on their followers that 'Home Rule was Rome Rule'.

In July 1920 the IRA shot dead Lt Colonel Brice Ferguson Smyth, who had earlier made an infamous speech in Listowel, where he said that the police were perfectly justified in shooting people who did not immediately put their hands up when challenged and that, if mistakes were made, policemen should not face court proceedings. When his body was taken to Banbridge, his home town, for burial, the UVF instigated the burning of Catholic-owned homes and property in the town. This violence spread to Dromore and Lisburn, with Catholics being forced out of work and out of their homes.

46. The gutted ruins of the parochial house following attacks on Catholic-owned
    property in Lisburn in August 1920. A disturbing feature is that the crowd in
    front (including women and children) is a loyalist one (note the Union Jack)
    clearly proud of their handiwork in the cold light of day. (Mooney Collection)

Violence was revisited on these communities the following month, when
RIC District Inspector Oswald Ross Swanzy was shot in Lisburn on a Sunday
morning as worshippers poured out from Lisburn Cathedral. Swanzy had
been implicated in the murder of Tomás MacCurtain, lord mayor of Cork and
commander of the IRA's Cork No. 1 Brigade. He had fled to the safety of the
strongly loyalist town of Lisburn. This was sectarianism at its most blatant, as
practically every Catholic-owned business in the town was burned to the ground
and the parochial house was totally destroyed. Those of the 1,000+ Catholic
population who could fled for their lives. Only seven ventured out to attend
Mass on the following Sunday. This attack lasted for three days and nights, and
it was not until September that attacks on isolated Catholic families petered
out. Many of those involved in these attacks were later to become members of
the Special Constabulary. When some were arrested for looting and arson, they
threatened the British government with organised attacks on Catholics in other
towns if they were charged and convicted. All charges were dropped.
    Some of the earliest manifestations of sectarianism were the reprisals carried
out by loyalists on innocent nationalists in the towns of Banbridge, Dromore and

Lisburn, and to a lesser extent Antrim and Newtownards. Similar attacks were carried out in Roslea, County Fermanagh, and Desertmartin, County Derry. In both cases the villages were practically razed, as Catholic-owned property was looted and burned by the Ulster Special Constabulary. The burning of Roslea, on 21 February 1921, was in reprisal for the attempted murder by the IRA of Constable George Lester as he opened his shop in the village. Revenge came

47. A burnt-out Catholic-owned shop in Bow Street, Lisburn, in August 1920. (Mooney Collection)

48. A Catholic-owned bicycle shop in Roslea, Co. Fermanagh, in the wake of the burning of the town by the Ulster Special Constabulary.

that evening when Specials and UVF men descended on Roslea, attacking the parochial house and burning ten nationalist-owned homes. The roads out of Roslea were filled with people carrying whatever possessions they could gather as they fled the flames that were engulfing the village. Only one person was to die in this attack, a UVF man named Finnegan, who was shot when he was using the butt of his rifle to break down a door: the rifle discharged, killing him.

The IRA avenged this attack on Roslea a month later, when up to sixteen homes of members of the 'B' Specials were targeted in a single night; three were killed. The unionist community saw this as a sectarian attack, as not all killed were Specials and one person, Sergeant Samuel Nixon, was shot dead after he had handed over his rifle in surrender.

The attack and the killings by 'Specials' in Desertmartin on 19 May 1922 was one of the worst sectarian incidents during this period. Two Specials started a small fire in a large four-storey mill in the village; the plan was to take credit for having discovered it, put it out and place the blame on the mainly nationalist population of the village. The fire, however, got out of control and the mill was gutted. The Specials responsible for setting the fire claimed to have seen two men running away from the scene, and this was sufficient excuse for Specials from the area and from nearby Magherafelt to loot and burn Catholic-owned homes and shops in Desertmartin. Where it was not possible to burn a house, because of adjacent Protestant neighbours, furniture and possessions were throw into the street and became part of a bonfire. While this mayhem was going on in the village, a number of Specials, in uniform, went to the homes of the Catholic McGeehan and Higgins families, took two sets of brothers out to a lonely country lane, lined them up against a ditch and riddled them with bullets. The Sunday after this slaughter four hearses brought their remains to Coolcalm church in Desertmartin, where they were interred in a single grave. At the inquest into their deaths the police admitted that they were respectable men who had never previously come to their notice.

Dominick Wilson, an IRA volunteer from Desertmartin, left the village when these killings took place. When he returned in July, four Specials called to his home at 2 am and took him from his bed to a nearby railway track, where he was beaten to death. It appeared that all four Specials took turns at shooting his body.

Such savagery was not confined to the Special Constabulary. In June 1921 the IRA decided to burn the home of retired clergyman Revd John Finlay, dean of Kildare and Leighlin, to prevent its being used to house Black and Tans. When Revd Finlay had retired in 1909 he and his wife had gone to live at Breckley House outside Bawnboy, County Cavan. The elderly couple was awakened on a Sunday morning at 1 am. Mrs Finlay and the servants were taken to a neighbour's house and ordered to remain there. She became alarmed when her husband did not join her and later ventured out to return to the house. By the light of her blazing home she found her eighty-year-old husband lying dead on the front lawn with his skull battered in. Reports later stated that he had been shot because he had objected to his home being burned.

In Belfast sectarian bitterness had been a fact of life for generations, as co-religionists chose to live together in their own districts in the narrow streets

49. Ulster Special Constabulary, on parade in nearby Newtownbutler in 1922 on 21 February 1921. (Mooney Collection, Michael McPhilips)

50. Volunteers of the IRA's 1st Battlion, 5th Northern Division, engaged in
weapons training. While the IRA did not set out with a sectarian agenda, as
the conflict went on they were drawn into sectarian killings, particularly in
Belfast. (Michael McPhilips)

of the industrialised city. During this period the head count of those killed
was not listed as unionist or nationalist but as Protestant or Catholic. From
the expulsion of Catholic workers from the Belfast shipyards and engineering
works in July 1920, when men had their shirts ripped open to see whether they
were wearing scapulars, so identifying them as Catholics, there was a litany
of attacks on the Catholic population in Belfast. These were not confined to
the burning of Catholic homes and businesses but included attacks on their
churches and on a convent. Such attacks led to reprisals and a 'tit-for-tat' spiral
of killings started.

When the gate lodge at St Matthew's Church in the Short Strand was set on
fire by loyalists and a crowd gathered to cheer as the building was consumed
in flames, the IRA threw a bomb into their midst, killing one man and injuring
forty-five others. The IRA also launched bullet and bomb attacks on tramcars
packed with shipyard workers. In one such incident in Corporation Street a
bomb was thrown into a tram, killing two men and seriously injuring other
passengers as part of the tram was blown apart.

In what was clearly a sectarian attack, the IRA held up a group of workmen
going to the massive Hughes and Dickson's flourmill in Divis Street. The men
were asked their religion and those who confirmed that they were Protestant
were fired at. One of the group died later in hospital after being shot, and another

was wounded. A similar shooting took place on 19 May 1922, when workmen in William Garret's cooperage in Little Patrick Street were lined up against a wall by up to nine armed men and asked their religion. Four Protestants—Thomas Boyd, Thomas Murphy, William Patterson and Thomas Maxwell—were separated from their Catholic workmates and shot as they stood against the wall. One was killed instantly, two died in hospital, and the fourth the following night. Such incidents served only to deepen the sectarian divide, as embittered family members saw reprisals as the only way forward.

There were similar atrocities on the loyalist side: for example, a bomb was thrown at a group of children playing in Weaver Street, a Catholic enclave close to a loyalist district. Two children died instantly and twenty-two suffered injuries, some of them horrific. It was not just civilians who were involved in sectarian attacks. The RIC and, it was suspected, a group of Specials led by District Inspector John William Nixon operated as a murder squad in Belfast. On 24 March 1922 four members of the McMahon family and a barman who worked for Owen McMahon were murdered in their home in Kinnaird Terrace, apparently in reprisal for the shooting dead of two Specials the previous day.

It is difficult when writing about this period to avoid being drawn into the 'what aboutery' of Irish history. Nevertheless, the facts are there; readers can make of them what they will.

Chapter 13

'Spies and informers beware!' IRA executions of alleged civilian spies during the War of Independence

Pádraig Óg Ó Ruairc

The 'intelligence war' was undoubtedly one of the most important aspects of the Irish War of Independence and remains one of the most controversial today. For the British, the best way to defeat the insurgency was to acquire accurate intelligence about IRA personnel, their

THE ARE AWAITING "THE DAY"
Non-Commissioned Officers of 'The Irish Brigade' in Germany who discarded the red and donned the Green.

51. Timothy Quinlisk (far right), a Catholic ex-soldier and former member of Casement's Irish Brigade, was one of the first civilians executed by the IRA as a British spy, in Ballyphehane, Co. Cork, in February 1920. (Joseph McGarrity Collection, Villanova University)

supply of arms and operations. Prior to the 1916 Rising they had relied on the RIC and the DMP, but the widespread closure of rural RIC barracks following IRA attacks, the success of Sinn Féin's police boycott and the consequent mass resignation of Irish-born constables meant that the British became increasingly dependent on civilians for information.

Given the previous role of spies and informers in compromising the insurrections of 1798 and 1867, the IRA was acutely aware of the importance of stopping the flow of intelligence to its enemy by identifying and eliminating British agents. As a guerrilla army relying on secrecy and mobility, the IRA was rarely in a position to punish suspected spies by holding them prisoner. Instead, the republicans inflicted a variety of other punishments on these suspects. Some received threatening notices; others suffered economic boycott or were forced into exile. In the most extreme cases republicans captured and killed civilians whom they claimed were spies and informers. The IRA killed a total of 184 civilians accused of spying during the War of Independence.

The intensity of the intelligence war and the number of related IRA killings varied widely throughout Ireland. The execution of suspected spies was almost exclusively a 'southern' phenomenon. Apart from a cluster in counties Armagh, Cavan and Monaghan, IRA executions of spies were almost unknown in Ulster. The largest number of IRA executions (sixty-six) occurred in Cork. The second-highest number was in Tipperary, where sixteen civilians accused of spying for the British forces were killed. The IRA in Dublin killed at least thirteen civilians for spying. These three counties alone accounted for more than half of such killings nationally. This is unsurprising, since these counties were the scene of intense IRA activity and were amongst the first districts to be placed under martial law by the British forces.

Nevertheless, the number of executions did not always correspond to the level of local IRA activity. The IRA in County Clare mounted a very strong military campaign that resulted in the deaths of forty-one British troops but only three executions of civilians accused of spying. By contrast, a desultory IRA campaign in County Meath inflicted just three fatalities on British forces yet killed four alleged spies. The only IRA execution to occur outside of Ireland during the conflict was the assassination of a British agent in Middlesex, England, although a number of later attempts were made after the 1921 Truce to kill suspected spies who had fled to the USA.

Given the potential threat posed by spies and informers, the execution of suspected British intelligence agents was a logical and necessary action from a republican perspective. It has repeatedly been suggested, however, that the IRA used the 'intelligence war' as a pretext to murder Protestants, ex-soldiers and Travellers. These accusations surfaced in the memoirs of British veterans published shortly after the conflict. Hugh Pollard, a former RIC press officer, claimed that these killings were primarily motivated by agrarianism and that those killed 'had nothing whatever to do with the authorities … these were private murders, possibly in pursuit of old faction feuds, but carried out under the all-embracing Irish cloak of patriotism'. The history of the British Army's 6th Division suggested a possible sectarian motive to these killings, noting that 'a large number of Protestant loyalists were murdered and labelled as spies' and that 'a regular murder campaign was instigated against Protestant loyalists and anyone who might be suspected of being an informer quite irrespective of whether he really was one or not'.

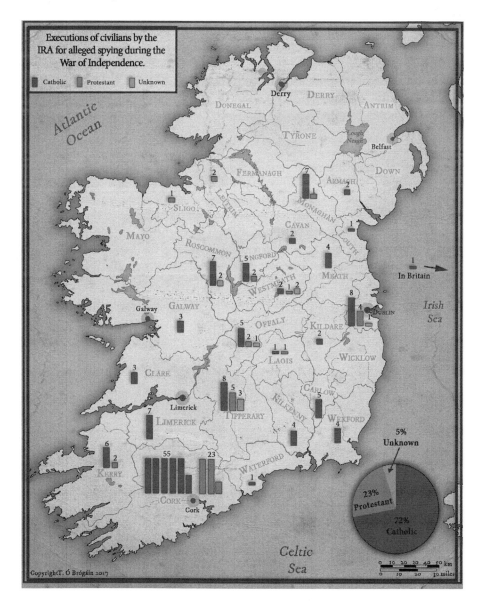

There has been an animated debate amongst historians as to the veracity of these claims. Much of the groundwork was laid by Peter Hart, who, taking Cork as a case-study, claimed that the majority of those executed for spying were innocent and that such killings often had more to do with prejudice against Protestants and ex-servicemen than genuine concerns about military security. Hart suggested that such killings were part of a national campaign of sectarian violence against Protestants that was tantamount to 'ethnic cleansing'. In fact, the overwhelming majority, 132 of the 184 civilians killed by the IRA as alleged spies (*c.* seventy-two per cent), were Catholic; just forty-three (*c.* twenty-three per cent) were Protestant. The execution of Protestants accused of spying was not widespread nationally. The IRA did not kill any civilians accused of spying in counties Antrim, Derry, Donegal, Down, Fermanagh, Mayo, Tyrone or Wicklow. Furthermore, Catholics accounted for all of those shot as spies by the IRA in counties Armagh, Carlow, Cavan, Clare, Galway, Kildare, Kilkenny, Limerick, Louth, Meath, Waterford and Wexford. On the face of it this belies the assertion that the IRA in these counties exploited the intelligence war as a pretext for sectarian murder or 'ethnic cleansing'.

The largest number of Protestant civilians killed by the IRA as alleged spies was in Cork, where twenty-one (*c.* thirty-two per cent) were Protestant. Although this figure appears to be disproportionately high, there were very large Protestant communities in Cork that were staunchly loyalist in politics and, consequently, may have been more willing to risk the IRA's wrath by assisting the British forces. The British Army's 'Record of the Rebellion in Ireland' reported that Protestant loyalists in west Cork had actively assisted the British forces 'in the Bandon Valley … there were many Protestant farmers who gave information … it proved almost impossible to protect these brave men many of whom were murdered'.

The IRA killed one alleged spy in County Sligo and a further two in County Leitrim—these areas are exceptional as the only counties where all of those killed as spies were Protestant. Even in these two counties, however, it is problematic to assume automatically that the three killings concerned were sectarian. The widow of one of the victims testified that her husband, William Latimer, a Protestant farmer, had supplied information to the RIC and she did not ascribe a sectarian motive to his killing. Lionel Curtis, a British government adviser who visited Ireland in 1921, reported that southern Irish Protestants did not complain of sectarian persecution and were targeted 'not by reason of their religion, but rather because they are under suspicion as loyalists'.

At least eight-eight of the civilians killed by the IRA as spies (approximately forty-eight per cent) were ex-servicemen. The vast majority of these had served in the British Army and the remainder were veterans of the Royal Navy. A further eight (*c.* four per cent) were ex-RIC constables. One of those killed, Hugh Duffy, was a member of the Ulster Special Constabulary, and another,

53. Alfred Reilly, manager of
Thompson's Bakery in
Cork, was shot by the IRA
as a suspected spy on 9
February 1921. Pinned to
his chest was an envelope on
which the words 'Beware of
the IRA' had been written
in pencil. Like a third of
the alleged spies killed in
County Cork, Reilly was a
Protestant.

William Nolan, had applied to join the RIC. Approximately two per cent of
those shot as spies were IRA Volunteers. At least eighty-six of those killed
(*c.* forty-six per cent) had no military or police service. Some historians, notably
Jane Leonard, have suggested that the IRA was prejudiced against Irishmen
who had served in the British Army. She contended that ex-soldiers 'weakened
the revolution's effectiveness by refusing to join Sinn Féin, subscribe to its
funds, or obey the rulings of its courts'.

In fact, however, former British soldiers were actively recruited by the IRA
and occupied important leadership positions within it. Such men included Emmet
Dalton, the IRA's director of training; Tom Barry, training officer for the West
Cork Brigade; Jim Tormey, commandant of the Athlone Brigade; and Ignatius
O'Neill, commander of the Mid-Clare Brigade. Far from being prejudiced against
ex-soldiers, the IRA valued and promoted them because of their military experience.
William Corrie, an ex-British soldier who joined the IRA's Dublin Brigade,
recalled: 'During my service with the IRA I met *hundreds* of ex-servicemen.'

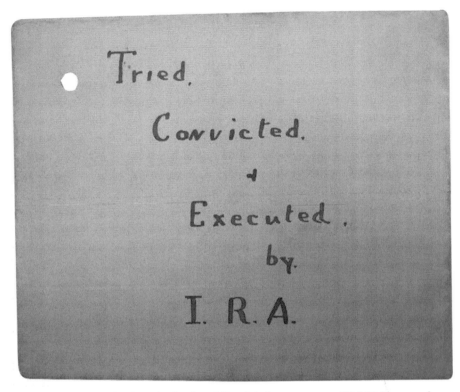

54. The label attached to the body of Patrick Larmour, an IRA Volunteer from Monaghan who 'broke' under British interrogation and was executed by his comrades.

Nevertheless, the IRA had reason to be suspicious of ex-soldiers with strong loyalist sympathies or those whose financial difficulties gave them an economic incentive to engage in intelligence work. Irishmen who had served in the British forces were more likely to suffer economic hardship than their British counterparts. Unemployment amongst ex-soldiers in post-war Ireland reached forty-six per cent compared to just ten per cent in Britain. The economic difficulties of ex-servicemen, coupled with their military training and previous loyal service to the British Crown, made them ideal candidates for recruitment by the British for counter-insurgency work. The British made a number of attempts to exploit ex-soldiers' associations to gather intelligence on the IRA. Whilst the IRA nationally killed a large number of ex-servicemen, including in Limerick and Cork city, the British were responsible for the majority of ex-soldiers killed in these areas.

It has also been suggested that the IRA exercised prejudice against tramps and Travellers during the conflict. Was this, perhaps, related to the practice of British agents, who often disguised themselves as such on intelligence-gathering missions? Kenneth Strong, a British intelligence officer stationed in Tullamore, travelled the countryside disguised 'as the owner of a small donkey cart' when meeting locals whom he had recruited as informers. Hugh McIvor, a Black and Tan stationed in Bandon, recalled that a senior RIC officer led a 'special squad' of RIC constables who 'all dressed like old farmers' whilst on intelligence-gathering operations. Given that British agents disguised themselves in this manner, is it any wonder that the IRA harboured deep suspicions about vagrants, a number of whom were killed as spies?

Only four of those executed by the IRA as suspected spies came from within their own ranks. One of these was Patrick Larmour, an IRA Volunteer from Monaghan who was arrested by the British and 'broke' under interrogation. After being released from custody, Larmour told his superior officers in the IRA what had happened. Although it is unlikely that he gave the British any significant information, he was shot as a spy. The execution of IRA Volunteers as alleged spies proved highly divisive in republican circles. Debate as to the guilt or innocence of Patrick D'Arcy, an IRA Volunteer shot as an alleged spy in west Clare, raged for decades after his death. James Dalton, an IRA officer in Limerick city, was shot as the result of an internal IRA feud. The allegation that Dalton was a spy seems to have been concocted after the killing, and a short time later Dáil Éireann took the unprecedented step of investigating Dalton's death and issuing a public statement declaring his innocence.

Just three women were killed by the IRA for spying, the most infamous incident being the execution of Mrs Maria Lyndsay. Mrs Lyndsay was abducted by the IRA in March 1921 because she had informed the British Army about an IRA ambush at Dripsey, County Cork. Acting on her information, the British Army had launched a surprise attack, capturing five IRA Volunteers who were later tried by courts martial and executed. The IRA had warned the British that they would kill Lyndsay if the republican prisoners were executed. They duly carried out their threat and buried her body in secret. Fr Shinnick, a Catholic priest who had assisted Mrs Lyndsay, was not killed. Although the killing of women was a taboo rarely broken, killing a clergyman of any denomination would have been even more controversial, and although the IRA knew of several clergymen, both Catholic and Protestant, who had gathered intelligence for the British, none of them were executed.

The majority of civilians killed by the IRA as suspected spies were shot dead. As a warning to others, their bodies were usually deposited in public places with an accompanying label reading 'Shot by IRA—spies and informers beware!' Traits of these killings included tying the condemned to a fixed post, execution by firing squad and the use of 'spy' labels mimicking contemporary British military practices. A few IRA units in counties Roscommon and Meath killed suspected spies by drowning rather than shooting, a bizarre method of execution never fully explained. Another unusual practice adopted by the IRA was the 'disappearance' of

55. Mrs Maria Lyndsay—one of just three women shot by the IRA for
spying—prior to her execution in January 1921, as re-enacted in TV3's 2013
documentary *In the Name of the Republic*. (Tile Films)

suspected spies, whose bodies were secretly buried instead of being labelled
and dumped in a public area for discovery. British forces were also known
to 'disappear' some of their victims, but it was far more common for the
IRA to do so. The practice appears to have been adopted in circumstances
where the IRA felt that the killing would not be approved of by the wider
community, such as the shooting of Mrs Lyndsay. It may also have been a
pragmatic measure to hide evidence of these killings.

The IRA tactic of hiding these bodies remains controversial, probably because
of similarities with those 'disappeared' by the Provisional IRA in the more recent
conflict in Northern Ireland. The practice, however, was relatively rare during
the War of Independence. Eunan O'Halpin's claim that approximately 200 of
the IRA's opponents were 'abducted, executed and ... secretly disposed of' is
undoubtedly a gross overestimate. Fewer than twenty-five of those executed
as spies during the War of Independence were 'disappeared' by the IRA; the
majority of their remains have yet to be recovered. Given that in most cases
there is no historical documentation publicly available that can conclusively
confirm whether those killed by the IRA as spies were in fact British agents, it
is likely that these killings will remain controversial, whether or not the victims
were 'disappeared'.

Chapter 14

'Murder stops play – eventually!': gentlemen of Ireland versus the military of Ireland, 3 June 1921

Barry Keane

As the 'Gentlemen of Ireland' had played only eight matches between 1910 and 1921, the War of Independence presented a golden opportunity to play decent opposition, with so many cricketing troops stationed here. A two-day match was arranged for the first weekend in June 1921 and, as always, College Park was the venue. A good crowd was guaranteed, as one of the greatest of all Irish cricketers, Bob Lambert, was taking part. Lambert had his own legion of adoring fans and both as a batsman and a bowler always entertained the crowd.

The two-day match was fixed to begin at 11 am on Friday 3 June to celebrate Warrior's Day and, like every other day that summer, the sun shone. A side had to lose all its batsmen twice to lose the match. For security, the ground was ringed

56. A cricket match at College Park, Trinity College, Dublin, c. 1900. The marquee to the right is roughly where Miss Kathleen Wright was shot on 3 June 1921. (NLI)

57. The view of the shooters over the wall along Nassau Street into College Park.

by troops in full battle dress. The military won the toss and decided to bat. They were soon in trouble, and after they lost their two top-class players for only nine runs they struggled to a total of 108. The equally famous Irish bowler Wenty Allen had taken five scalps in a row. Lambert and John Crawford had added 127 runs to Ireland's score, bringing their total to 266 runs in response, and they were well on their way to a very easy win by tea at 5 pm. The Irish would have a whole day on 4 June to bowl the army out and famously win the match. If the army survived, the match would be a draw. There was a good crowd in the morning but the park really filled up in the afternoon, as government staff (many of whom were English) finished work early on the Friday to watch it. The crowd were in good spirits as Lambert and Crawford smashed the English bowlers to all parts of the ground. The Army had underestimated the challenge presented by the Irish, and the local fans were enjoying beating the British at their own game.

At 5.30 pm, just as the military band was leaving the field after the tea break, shots rang out from the railings on the Nassau Street side of the ground. The band and the Army players, who were fielding, threw themselves to the ground. Not knowing what was going on, the two batsmen looked on in stunned disbelief before they too were hauled to the ground by the soldiers. According to the *Irish Times*, two men had cycled up 'and carefully placed their machines against the kerbstone. They advanced towards the railings and, producing revolvers, fired them in the direction of the players. They then put their revolvers in their pockets, remounted their bicycles, and rode away.'

The incident was over so quickly that most of the crowd had not even reacted before the players started to pick themselves up and check whether everyone was unhurt. The umpires and captains decided to carry on. On the face of it, even if none of the military were killed, the IRA had pulled off a 'spectacular'. Before another ball was bowled, the game was interrupted by another disturbance from the Nassau Street side of the ground. One of the spectators had collapsed. Miss Kathleen Wright, a Trinity student, had gone to the game with her fiancé, George Hubert Ardill, son of a clergyman in Sligo. The *Irish Times* reported that 'Miss Kathleen Alexanderson Wright received a bullet wound in the back, and there was a corresponding exit wound in the breast, from which blood flowed freely'. The official report in the *Irish Times* reported her last words as 'I have such a pain in my chest' before she collapsed and died. Another lady spectator sitting next to her had been shot in the arm, possibly by the same bullet. George Ardill told her inquest that three doctors had attended her and 'one had told him there was no hope. He [George] had accompanied her to hospital where he was told she was dead'.

Another witness identified where she was sitting in the park: 'He went out immediately, and ran to where a crowd was collecting inside the park railings opposite the Kildare Street Club. A few of his friends told him what had happened and said that the shots came through the railings.' Incredibly, after the shooting the cricket match resumed. The provost of Trinity, John Henry Bernard, came to the ground, however, and the match was then abandoned. The official report ended with the comment that 'The attackers made good their escape'.

There matters rested until the release of the Bureau of Military History (BMH) statements in 2003. While it had been known since 2000 that Paddy O'Connor and Jim McGuiness had done the shooting, no details from the IRA side had been found. With the release of the BMH documents Paddy O'Connor's version of events was now in the public domain:

> During the summer of 1921 a cricket match was held in Trinity College between the Gentlemen of Ireland and the Military. We were instructed to stop this match taking place. Our instructions were that we were to go down to the vicinity of Trinity College and fire into the grounds. Jimmy McGuinness and myself cycled down as the match was just starting. From a position behind the boundary wall of Trinity College at Lincoln Place, the two of us opened fire in the general direction of the players. After the first couple of rounds were fired, a lady spectator jumped up from one of the seats and got killed by a stray shot. The match was not proceeded with.

That, it seems, was that.

MURDER IN COLLEGE PARK.

CRICKET TEAM FIRED AT.

YOUNG LADY KILLED.

ATTACKERS' ESCAPE.

A shocking outrage took place yesterday afternoon at Trinity College Park, Dublin, as a result of which a young lady student has lost her life.

The occasion was one of festivity and enjoyment in the College Park. A cricket match in connection with Warriors' Day was in progress. The teams were, the Gentlemen of Ireland versus the Military of Ireland. The general belief is that the latter were the objects of the murderous attack which resulted so tragically.

The cricket match, like all similar events held in the College Park, attracted a very large and fashionable crowd. The weather was delightfully fine, and the hot sun induced many to seek the shade of the trees bordering the beautiful grounds.

Interest in the match was very keen, and the play had reached, perhaps, its most attractive stage at 5.30, when suddenly the spectators were startled by a rapid fusillade of revolver fire from the direction of the railings on the Nassau street side of the ground. Seven shots rang out in quick succession, and the spectators rushed for shelter. When the military, who were fielding at the time, were seen lying prone on the ground it was feared that the shots of the assailants had taken effect, but

In a statement by the All Brothers they say that so long as they are associated with the non-co-operation movement they shall not directly or indirectly advocate violence.

VICTIM OF TRINITY TRAGEDY

GRIEF-STRICKEN FAMILY

The body of Miss K. A. Wright, the victim of the Trinity College tragedy, will be brought to England to-day or to-morrow for burial at Brixton.

Mr. Ruthven A. Wright, brother, who is also a student of Trinity, travelled to London by night mail on Friday to convey the tragic news to his parents. When a representative of the P.A. called at All Saints Vicarage, Clapham Park, he found the family overwhelmed with grief.

Miss Kathleen Wright.

Mr. Wright said he knew nothing whatever of the details. He had been out rowing, and on his return to the college learnt of the tragedy from Miss Wright's fiance, who was unable to say very much, as he was in a state of collapse. Mr. Wright explained that Mr. Ardill was formerly an officer in the West Kent Regt., but now a student at Trinity.

FATHER PROSTRATE.

The deceased's father intended to travel to Dublin on Sat. night to bring back the body, but he was prostrate, and was advised not to make the journey. Throughout Sat. messages of sympathy poured into the Vicarage, and there was a steady stream of people anxious to offer their condolences to the family, which is held in high esteem.

Rev. Mr. Wright told "Lloyd's News" that his family had been associated with Trinity for 4 or 5 generations. "It seems clear," he said, "that the attack was on the military, but though my daughter's fiance is a strong loyalist he is not in the army. To my mind the Government do not sufficiently protect Irish loyalists."

Sir Almroth Wright, the well-known physician who attacked the Women's Suffrage movement in 1912, is uncle of Miss Wright, and Rev. C. H. H. Wright, the famous Hebrew scholar, was her grandfather.

The cricket match between Gentlemen and Military of Ireland, was abandoned owing to the tragedy.

MONEY.

Any amount to lend on Valuable Property without delay at the most privately situated offices in Dublin. The first-class Pawn Office, 85 MARLBOROUGH ST.

59. One of the shooters, Col. Padraig O'Connor, in National Army uniform in Beggars Bush barracks, 1922 (Diarmuid O'Connor). Padraig ('Paddy') O'Connor was a veteran of the 1916 Rising, the War of Independence and the Civil War. He served under Michael Collins and held the rank of lieutenant in the 4th Dublin Brigade. In 1923 he was promoted to colonel in the National Army (he was one of the officers who took over Beggars Bush Barracks from the British) and was appointed director of training in May 1923. He instigated the formation of a completely Irish-speaking battalion in the Irish Army in 1924. In 1928 he became governor of Limerick Prison. He returned to army service during the Second World War. He died suddenly in 1953, aged fifty-two.

The newspapers suggested that Kathleen Wright was English, but her father, Revd Ernest Alexanderson Wright, was from Ireland and was the vicar of All Saints in Clapham Park, London. His brothers included Eric Wright, supreme justice of the Seychelles, General Henry Wright, who fought in the Boer War and the Great War, Sir Almroth Wright, who created the typhoid inoculation, and Sir Charles Wright, assistant librarian at the National Library of Ireland. Her grand-uncle had been a professor of botany in Trinity. The Wright family had come to Ireland with Cromwell and had remained at the top of Irish legal, academic and military society for generations. She was one of the fourth generation to have been educated at Trinity. Kathleen Wright's death struck right at the heart of the loyal, unionist and mostly Protestant community at play. While the military had been the target, the recklessness of firing across the spectators smacks of Bloody Sunday and the Crown forces' attack on Croke Park in November 1920. George accompanied her body to London; after a funeral service conducted by Canon Ardill, she was buried in Wandsworth cemetery on 8 June. She was twenty-one.

Chapter 15

From the outside in: the international dimension to the Irish Civil War

Bill Kissane

The German sociologist Max Weber was noted for his interest in how the geopolitical position of states affected their domestic politics. Revolutions, civil wars and *coups d'état* often came 'from the outside in', as changes in the international arena weakened central authorities and exposed dominant élites to challenges from below. In contrast, much of the recent literature on the Irish Civil War stresses the primacy of internal factors—the existence of rival traditions within Sinn Féin, de Valera's rejection of the treaty or the militarist traditions of the IRA. The shock of civil war forced many to revise assumptions about the character of Irish nationalism, and some concurred with the title of an RTÉ documentary that the Civil War was an expression of 'the madness within'. Yet the Irish Civil War clearly occurred as part of a general wave of state formation in inter-war Europe, which saw intense fighting break out immediately after independence in Finland, the three Baltic states and Hungary (if not Czechoslovakia). Since drawing a line between domestic and international politics in any of these cases is impossible, any study of the Irish case also has to relate the 'madness within' to what Joe Lee called 'the madness without'.

The Anglo-Irish treaty of 1921 established the Irish Free State as a dominion of the British Empire. Its constitutional status was to be analogous to that of Canada, and a Boundary Commission would establish the exact border separating northern from southern Ireland, if the northern parliament 'opted out' of the Free State. To pro-treatyites, it was an honourable compromise, dictated by military necessity, but one that could serve as 'a stepping stone' to full independence. To anti-treatyites, it was a sell-out, one that achieved neither unity nor independence, and which tied the new state as closely to the British Empire as the Act of Union had done in 1801. Given the broken promises of the past, why trust in Britain's capacity to deal with Ireland in a generous way in the future? Others argued that the agreement was an international treaty, and that dominion status was a guarantee of good treatment in itself.

In 1966 Professor T. D. Williams wrote that the experience of a nationalist movement falling out over a treaty with a departing colonial power was not

60. Republican poster (of Sir James Craig?) attributed to Countess Markievicz. (National Library of Ireland)

unique to Ireland. Yet the typical pattern of decolonisation in the twentieth century had been for independence to proceed peacefully in two stages—a treaty of association followed by full independence. The Irish were the only ones to fight a civil war specifically over that formula. This had much to do with the international background to the treaty split. By 1918 European politics had been radicalised by the Great War, by the democratisation of the suffrage that followed from it, and by the promise of self-determination for small nations made by the Allies during the war. In January 1919 Sinn Féin convened an elected parliament in Dublin, declared a thirty-two-county republic, and appealed for a hearing at Versailles. Its case for recognition was intended for the American audience, and assumed that Ireland was (like the Czechs or the Poles) an 'ancient' European nation, whose status could only be confirmed by international recognition.

Yet its assumption that Irish self-determination necessitated leaving the empire was not shared by the Irish diaspora, and Irish American opinion soon became split on the issue of 'the isolated republic'. Realists pointed out that the principle of self-determination was intended to apply only to the territory of the defeated empires, not to that of the United Kingdom. Majorities in the north-east of Ireland had voted for unionist MPs in 1918, and the electorate returned the Conservative Party with a large majority to Westminster. In the absence of Irish MPs, both combined to partition Ireland in 1920, bringing into question the wisdom of Sinn Féin's abstentionist policy. Lloyd George had been under little pressure to hear the Irish case at Versailles, and moved towards negotiation only in 1921. By that time he knew that the Americans would support an offer of dominion status for Ireland and that world opinion would support him in this proposal.

As the unity of Sinn Féin floundered on the rocks of this new imperial partnership, arguments for and against the treaty reflected the geopolitical dimension. Michael Collins is remembered primarily as a realist. In international relations theory, realists assume that self-interest and force determine relations between states. As a result, no international order is ever fixed, and the linchpin of Collins's case for the treaty was his view that it provided 'the freedom to achieve freedom'. In contrast, de Valera's inflexibility on the Treaty has been ascribed to his intellectualism, but it reflected the same idealism that supposedly inspired Woodrow Wilson's vision of a new world order. Collins had grasped the real nature of that order in 1921, while de Valera's preference for a republic 'externally associated' with the empire became practicable only after 1945. Professor Alfred O'Rahilly of University College Cork described de Valera's formula as 'ingenious, but premature'. This comment points to why a treaty of association created a deep split within Ireland, but not elsewhere. In 1921 the British Empire was very much a going concern, whereas after 1945 anti-colonial nationalists could accept free association first, secure in the knowledge that history was on course to full independence.

After the Dáil had voted in favour of the treaty, and once the IRA occupied Dublin's Four Courts on 13 April, it is often assumed that the divide was too wide to bridge peacefully. De Valera had played a crucial role in keeping moderates and militants united before 1921, but his opposition to the treaty now deepened the divide. In April 1922 an IRB peace initiative led to the formation of a Dáil peace committee to discuss maintaining unity in the coming election, but after eleven meetings the committee could not produce a joint report. The pro-treaty delegates wanted it to acknowledge that the majority of the people were in favour of the Treaty, while the anti-Treaty delegates wanted it understood that nothing was being decided in the election. Despite standing on a common platform in the 'pact election' on 16 June, this basic difference of outlook resurfaced afterwards. Pro-treatyites thought that the election gave them a mandate to implement the treaty. Their opponents thought the mandate was for coalition government and peace. The issue of democracy had proven 'irrepressible'.

The outbreak of civil war on 28 June could thus be seen as the product of a process of ideological polarisation over the issue of majority rule. In the interests of maintaining unity, Sinn Féin had fudged its constitutional differences in 1917, and the absence of a normal political life, with properly contested elections and a free press, meant that the differences were suppressed until peaceful conditions returned. The fact that both press and pulpit advocated accepting the treaty in 1922, and that forty per cent of the electorate voted for third parties in the June election, undermined the electoral monopoly that Sinn Féin had achieved in 1918. The title of Tom Garvin's 1996 work *1922: The Birth of Irish Democracy* sought to encapsulate this dynamic. The response of the anti-treaty IRA—through threatening to prevent the election from taking place, for example—suggested that they had a vested interest in preventing a return to normal conditions.

A key precondition for civil war is often the polarisation into two coherent groups of what was in Sinn Féin's case a rather loose and faction-ridden movement. Yet this condition was not realised in Ireland before June 1922, and British pressure ensured that it ultimately was. The second Dáil continued to assemble until June and would meet to dissolve itself on 30 June. Sinn Féin had committed itself to establishing a coalition government on 1 July and never formally renounced the terms of the Collins/de Valera electoral pact. The anti-Treaty IRA itself was divided between the garrison in Dublin's Four Courts and the larger southern divisions of the IRA, who retained their belief in the coalition idea up to the election. Since May 1922 negotiations had been going on between both these groups and the Provisional Government's Ministry of Defence, and their fate was inextricably linked to the coalition plan. In the background was the worsening situation in Northern Ireland, and both sides of the IRA had agreed to a secret offensive across the border in May. Two attempts by Collins to get Sir James Craig to reform the Northern Ireland government had already failed, and it was a northern delegation that finally convinced Collins to agree to the electoral pact with de Valera on 20 May.

Collins was the pivotal figure. Since his justification of the treaty had been based on an acknowledgement of *force majeure*, his commitment to the 'majority rule' principle was equivocal. His constitution committee had met seventeen times since January, and drafts B and C would specifically allow for anti-treaty

61. Michael Collins by Leo Whelan—remembered primarily as a realist. (OPW)

ministers in a coalition government. When the two sides met in conference on 25 May, however, Churchill insisted that all Irish ministers had to sign acceptance of the treaty, as was prescribed by article 17. Earlier that month Churchill had warned Collins that 'everyone of us will swing round with any scrap of influence we can command against a republic or any inroad upon the treaty structure'. Yet rather than vetoing the pact, the British government insisted that the new constitution conform to the treaty, and the final draft symbolised its authority in an emphatic manner. The text finally chosen, based on draft A, prescribed a

British-style cabinet bound by the rule of collective ministerial responsibility. This meant that anti-treaty ministers could not agree on internal policy while disagreeing on foreign relations, as was envisaged in draft C. Since the fate of the pact was inextricably linked to that of the constitution, there was no way the two sides could form a coalition government.

The trigger for civil war was the assassination of Field Marshal Sir Henry Wilson on 22 June and Lloyd George's subsequent demand that the occupation of the Four Courts no longer be tolerated. Arguments over what prompted the shelling of the Four Courts on 28 June would continue for decades to come. Kevin O'Higgins believed that civil war was inevitable because the 'mutineers' were about to carry out 'a *coup d'état*' that would plunge the country back into a power struggle with Britain. On 14 June the IRA executive had resolved to take 'whatever action may be necessary to maintain the Republic against British aggression'. The anti-treatyites, in contrast, saw British pressure as the decisive variable: one document cited a speech made by L. Worthington Evans, secretary of state for war and a treaty signatory, on 29 June, in which he stated that the British government had told the provisional government that they had to govern or simply go. If the pact had been adhered to, and if the provisional government had stood up to Britain over the constitution, republicans believed that civil war could have been avoided. In 1936 de Valera published an article in *The Catholic Bulletin* claiming that it was actually his opponents who had carried out 'an executive *coup d'état*' in June 1922.

Once the battle for Dublin had resulted in a clear-cut victory for the Free State army, the uncertain course of developments before July gave way to a much more decisive pattern. The fall of the Four Courts, the IRA's retreat to the countryside and their failure to defend the 'Munster Republic' in conventional hostilities have been attributed to the strategic superiority of the Free State leadership. The naval landings at Cork and Kerry are good examples, but the key variable was the inequality of power resources between the two sides. All irregular civil wars are characterised by 'asymmetry', in that the insurgents employ 'the weapons of the weak' against an army they cannot defeat conventionally. This asymmetry was especially pronounced in Ireland, however. The massive supply of arms provided by the British government, and the ability of the provisional government (supported by the banks) to finance an army of over 50,000 men, meant that an IRA military victory was possible only in the early stages of the war. But the IRA chief-of-staff, Liam Lynch, was still contemplating negotiations up to the middle of July, and many IRA men simply went home rather than fight a civil war.

Insurgencies not buoyed up by early military successes often fade away. Peter Hart has suggested that in Cork the number of IRA men had dwindled to one tenth of their pre-treaty strength by October 1922. Given the precedent established in 1916, the scale of resistance to the Free State was unimpressive.

62. Northern Ireland prime minister Sir James Craig—in the background was the worsening situation in Northern Ireland. Two attempts by Collins to get Craig to reform the Northern Ireland government had already failed. (George Morrison)

The one realistic war aim of the IRA was to force the capitulation of the Provisional Government, but behind that lay the question of how to deal with the Ulster unionists and the British Army. On 11 February 1923, a demoralised Frank Barrett from Clare wrote to Lynch, asking how they were going to defeat England if they could not unite with the National Army. On the other hand, by resorting to guerilla tactics in the autumn, the IRA had returned to what they

63. The Treaty delegates in London the day after the signing. (George Morrison)

knew best, and tested the nerve of a provisional government that had lost its best military leader in Collins on 22 August. British intelligence reports predicted that W. T. Cosgrave, the new chairman of the Provisional Government, would not be able to see the fighting through to the end, but a chief paradox of the war would be that civilians like Cosgrave would prove more adept at fighting than the military men.

This paradox can be explained with reference to the advantage of incumbency in conflict situations. With a nascent state apparatus at its disposal, the provisional government showed a clearer sense of purpose than the IRA, and consistently refused to compromise on issues touching on the authority of the state, such as entering into negotiations without prior IRA decommissioning. The IRA's retreat to the countryside had allowed the Provisional Government to project itself as the 'protector' of society, while the newspapers were required to refer to the IRA as 'bands' or 'bodies'. Any new state that bases its authority primarily on its 'protective' role will inevitably strengthen the position of the dominant social groups, and the army quickly became involved in suppressing the labour and agrarian unrest spreading through the countryside in 1922–3. Guerilla tactics also gave credence to the Catholic Church's proclamation, read out at all Masses on 22 October, that killing national soldiers was 'murder in the eyes of God'. Anti-treaty Catholics failed to get the Vatican to reverse its policy of excommunicating IRA men, and the IRA executive also tried unsuccessfully to import pieces of artillery from Germany in the spring of 1923, which Lynch hoped would turn the course of the war. IRA columns could hold out in the mountainous terrain of the south-west, but had to weigh the benefits of further resistance against the government's execution policy. In 1933 Frank Aiken recalled that the fact that the government had already selected additional IRA prisoners to be executed, given the slightest pretext, played a major role in forcing his side to call a ceasefire on 30 April.

Yet de Valera's attempt to turn military defeat into political victory through negotiations in May 1923 proved unsuccessful. After Collins's death the government had rejected initiatives aimed at restoring the unity of the IRA. Indirect negotiations failed because the government was unwilling to exchange the abolition of the oath for IRA decommissioning. In 1933 Aiken recalled that when de Valera's decommissioning proposals were sent to IRA units and prisoners, not a single protest was made to the IRA executive, which had unanimously backed its terms. On 24 May, however, Kevin O'Higgins wrote to Cosgrave emphasising that 'the present government has no intention of jeopardising the important benefits of the treaty position, which makes the taking of the oath a condition precedent to taking a seat in the Oireachtas'. After ten months of civil war, the treaty settlement was more secure than it would have been under almost any other outcome to the split. Cosgrave and his colleagues had absorbed one aspect of the realist case for the treaty—recognition of external constraints—while putting the 'stepping stone' approach on hold.

64. The fall of the Four Courts. Once the battle for Dublin had resulted in a clear-cut victory for the Free State army, the uncertain course of developments before July gave way to a much more decisive pattern. (George Morrison)

The abolition of the Dáil courts, the abandonment of Griffith's protectionist economic policies and the Boundary Commission fiasco all suggested a successor regime that would protect vital British interests.

Yet as the international crisis deepened in the 1920s, and as the Commonwealth itself moved towards greater equality in 1931, the realist case for the treaty would be vindicated. After 1932 de Valera whittled away at the settlement, using a rationale articulated by Collins a decade earlier. His opponents would never forgive him for this. Yet in 1922 de Valera had articulated a position on the treaty consistent with the philosophy of Sinn Féin and with prevailing international norms. The Civil War had come from the 'outside in', and, despite the Irish obsession with personalities, there is no evidence that he or Collins could have stopped it, short of abandoning their basic positions on the Treaty. Most remarkably of all, the British government would soon lose interest in Ireland, leaving a troubled legacy for which it felt little responsibility. In 1922 Winston Churchill and his colleagues had ensured that the process of ideological polarisation would reach its logical conclusion in civil war. They had deemed a coalition government unacceptable, created the conditions that made that government impossible, and then succeeded in largely obliterating the memory of their own role in the process.

Chapter 16

The Clones affray, 1922: massacre or invasion?

Robert Lynch

O n Saturday 11 February 1922 at the railway station in the small border
town of Clones, County Monaghan, a gun battle took place between the
IRA and a party of Ulster Special Constabulary. It resulted in five deaths,
including four of the Specials and the local IRA commandant. Numerous other
combatants and civilians were wounded. The events at Clones were inevitably
interpreted in radically different ways by both unionists and nationalists,
occurring as they did amidst the establishment of two new administrations in
Ireland. For unionists the Clones incident was a 'massacre' ruthlessly planned
and carried out by the IRA. Nationalists tended to paint the Specials' arrival
in Clones as akin to some form of invasion of Free State territory enhanced by
the brutal and unprovoked murder of the local IRA commander. What was the
truth behind these conflicting claims?

What later became known as the 'Clones affray' was an indirect consequence of
Michael Collins's confused early attempts to impede the establishment of Northern
Ireland. From the signing of the Anglo-Irish treaty in late December 1921 until the
outbreak of civil war six months later Collins would use every means at his disposal,
both military and political, to make partition unworkable. The first test of his new
policy came about almost by accident. On 14 January 1922, the same day that the
Provisional Government was established in Dublin, senior officers of the IRA's
Monaghan-based 5th Northern Division, including the divisional commandant
Dan Hogan, were arrested at Dromore, County Tyrone, en route to Derry City.
Ostensibly they were journeying as part of a Gaelic football team to take part in
the Ulster championship final. In reality this served as a front for a reconnaissance
mission aimed at eventually releasing three IRA men imprisoned in Derry Gaol
who were due to be hanged on 9 February. Later Eoin O'Duffy, chief-of-staff of
the pro-treaty IRA, indicated that he believed the Clones affray was due principally
'to the evident intention of the Northern government to hang the three Derry
prisoners' and the anger and instability this caused in border areas.

With the split in IRA ranks over the treaty now growing alarmingly Collins
seized on the opportunity these arrests provided for demonstrating his new
hard-line policy to those who had lost faith in his republican credentials. On the
night of 7–8 February, by way of retaliation, the IRA raided across the border

65. A Northern Ireland customs post near Newry c. 1922. Such posts became
    virtual armed camps with the IRA's increased activity along the border in
    early 1922. (PSNI)

in large numbers, concentrating particularly on the Clogher Valley in the south
of County Tyrone and the Enniskillen area. This co-ordinated attack involved
carloads of Monaghan, Longford and Leitrim IRA men who, after cutting local
communications and burning various properties, kidnapped over forty local
unionists and fled back across the border into County Monaghan.

The kidnapping raids had been planned by a shadowy new body called the
Ulster Council, which was established by Collins in early January 1922. Its aim was
to co-ordinate IRA activity in the six counties and along the border. This highly
secretive organisation acted under the auspices of the IRB, of which Collins was
President of the Supreme Council. He was joined at its head by Eoin O'Duffy and
Richard Mulcahy, and it was this IRB triumvirate that would be responsible for
organising the extensive IRA attacks in the north over the following six months.

Collins' determination to halt the executions of the Derry prisoners had
gone even further, sending two of his 'squad' to England to assassinate the two
hangmen who were to execute the prisoners; however, they had already left for
Ireland. At this point Clones became the centre of frenetic IRA activity. The
town itself contained the 5th Northern Divisional headquarters and lay within
a few miles of both the Tyrone and Fermanagh borders. Its strategic position
meant also that it had become the headquarters of the Ulster Council, within
easy reach of both Aiken and MacEoin's commands in Armagh and Longford
respectively. Both geographically and politically Clones lay at the centre of a
political storm that would soon erupt on its very doorstep.

While diplomatic efforts to release the 'Monaghan footballers' continued
apace, the local situation became extremely tense. In response to the kidnappings,

Specials poured into border areas. Bridges were blown and all but major roads were mined or trenched. The Specials set up checkpoints at the remaining border crossings and local farms were abandoned by their owners. A stalemate ensued and both sides exchanged fire across the now fortified border areas. It was against this backdrop that at around 5.15 pm on Saturday 11 February the ill-fated train containing the Specials arrived at Clones station. The party itself consisted of nineteen uniformed 'A' Specials led by Sergeant William Dougherty. Six of the constables were armed. They had left Newtownards via Belfast earlier in the day. Their final destination was Enniskillen where they were to reinforce the local USC platoons as part of the wider build up of forces along the Monaghan border. It certainly was a provocative route to choose, especially when one considers that the British army had evacuated Clones only days before to concentrate at the Curragh and Dublin. The clumsy choice of route did cause some consternation after the event although no evidence exists to suggest it involved any sinister motives, some kind of administrative blunder being the favoured interpretation.

On arrival at Clones, Sergeant Dougherty gathered the six-man armed party together on the platform. The rest of the men made their way to the buffet. One or two others strolled about the station mingling with civilians and kicking their heels until the train arrived. No IRA men appeared to be present at the station, although Constable John Guiness recalls noticing 'some suspicious looking young men on the platform all the time'. It is likely that at least one of these young men was responsible for alerting the IRA to the presence of the Specials and thus inadvertently turning an innocent journey into a tragic confrontation. Meanwhile in the IRA's divisional headquarters at the workhouse in Clones, battalion commandant Matt Fitzpatrick had recently arrived with some other officers. Fitzpatrick responded rapidly to the news of the Specials' arrival. Quickly arming themselves, he and three other officers leapt into a car and headed for the station, informing others to gather more men and follow him up as soon as possible. They sped off, covering the short distance to the railway station within minutes.

Back at the station the Specials were preparing to leave. The Enniskillen train had arrived and some of the party had taken their seats while others dawdled on the platform and drifted towards their carriages. As the last half-dozen or so Specials climbed aboard the train, Special Constable Peter Martin recalls that one of the railway porters came to the door of his compartment and pointing to the recently arrived IRA officers said 'They have it in for you boys'. Fitzpatrick and his three officers had just entered the main door of the station. Revolver in hand, he walked to the engine to stop the train from leaving. IRA lieutenant Patrick Rooney recalls the events as follows: 'When we got on the platform we turned towards the engine as the train was due to start. We then saw the engine was not attached. We turned back towards the rear of the train. Commandant Fitzpatrick was leading the men down the platform. I was behind him. On reaching the first compartment where there were Specials the commandant shouted 'Hands up! Surrender', immediately there was a shot from the compartment and Commandant Fitzpatrick dropped dead in front of me'.

It was never established who fired this fatal shot and the issue of which side had initiated the violence would become the subject of bitter argument over the following weeks with both sides claiming vociferously that they were the innocent victims of an unprovoked attack. However, what followed these few disputed seconds is more certain. Fitzpatrick, shot in the head with a single bullet, fell dead between two carriages. Immediately the situation exploded into chaos. The IRA, now numbering around twenty, dived for cover and a hail of bullets was fired at the Specials' carriages. An anonymous witness relates the chilling scene as follows: 'After we had been seated about two minutes shots suddenly rang out, about six being fired into our carriage in quick succession, one of the bullets flashing across my face and grazing my hat. I could hear shots being discharged all over the train mingled with the yells and screams of the men in the other carriages. I heard one man appeal for mercy, and another call for his mother.'

Frederick Browne of Enniskillen recalled seeing several individuals jumping out of the train on the opposite side only to be held up by an armed IRA man who forced them back into the carriages where the main attack was taking place. Hector Jeffers, a trooper in the Inniskilling Dragoons, who was in a compartment with one of the Specials, stated:

I heard the thud of a bullet coming through the woodwork of the carriage, a few minutes after this the special constable, said 'I am hit', and when I looked round he was bleeding from the mouth. His eyes closed and I think he died in a few minutes.

The scene on the platform was chaotic. Some of the Specials caught in the open attempted to surrender only to be raked with machine gun fire, whilst others either fled or returned fire from the wrecked carriages. By all accounts Constable Robert MacMahon was the first Special to be killed. Three others were to follow: Sergeant Dougherty and Constables James Lewis and William McFarland. The train had been riddled with bullets, concentrated mainly on carriage 85 where the Specials were located. Countless civilians were wounded including Patrick Crumley, the former Nationalist MP for South Fermanagh. Eight other Specials were wounded to varying degrees. Constable John Cummings was hit by machine gun fire below the waist and as a result lost his right leg. Constable George Lendrum had six machine gun bullets in him but somehow survived. Others escaped unscathed, although most, like Albert Lyttle, were very lucky. His cap was knocked off by a bullet and another passed harmlessly through his tunic.

The IRA, now arriving in large numbers, gave orders for everybody to leave the train. The civilians were separated from the remaining Specials of whom only three were unwounded. An anonymous witness related his view

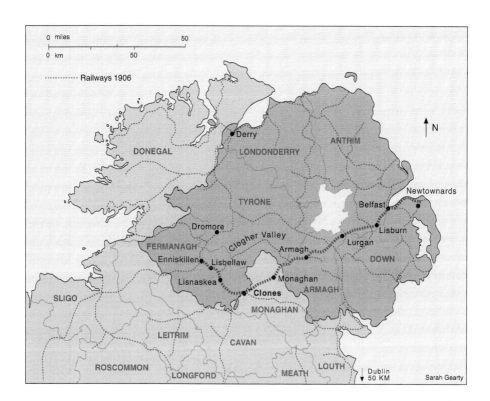

of the terrible aftermath: 'A number of passengers were ordered to clear the dead and wounded out of the carriages. The victims, numbering upward of 20 were carried from carriages and laid prostrate in the ladies waiting room. The passengers having completed the gruesome work of clearing the carriages, returned with their faces, hands and clothing saturated with blood.'

The train itself left forty-five minutes late, around 6.40 pm. Despite the IRA allowing the civilians to continue their journey, it appears that only a few took this opportunity. In Clones itself IRA units from counties Monaghan, Fermanagh and Cavan poured into the Clones area. They extinguished street lamps and put out lights in local shops and houses. Tensions were running extremely high. In Monaghan town a local girl was shot accidentally by the IRA around 9 pm. When the train finally arrived at Lisbellaw, its carriages wrecked and covered in blood, the local population exploded in riotous anger.

Despite the small scale of the Clones affray and the fact that it is now almost forgotten, at the time it threatened to spark off a major confrontation between North and South. The first ominous move in this rapid escalation was the immediate suspension of British troop evacuations from the Free State and the intensification of violence on the border between the IRA and the USC. James Craig, the Northern premier, demanded permission from Churchill to send 5,000 troops over the border to rescue the kidnapped loyalists and to occupy a portion of Free State territory for

67. Police on patrol in the York Street area of Belfast c. 1922 after a night of
    rioting. (PSNI)

each loyalist still held in the South. Churchill, worried over the rapid escalation of
the situation and fearful for the stability of the Provisional Government in the south
if such an invasion took place, refused the request outright.

In order to appease Craig, three extra battalions of British troops were sent
to the North and a border commission was established on 16 February to act
as an ad-hoc peace keeping agency offering arbitration in any future border
disputes. The commission itself achieved very little and eventually faded out of
existence by the end of April. A British officer claimed that one of the Specials
told him that they had received orders to fire on any vehicle flying the border
commission's blue and white flag. General Macready, commander-in-chief
of British forces in Ireland, was skeptical from the start: 'To those who knew
anything of the two component parts of the commission, the IRA and Ulster
representatives, the scheme was foredoomed to failure, though no doubt it
looked very attractive in Whitehall. From the first, in spite of the loyal efforts
of the British officers, the whole affair was a farce'.

On 21 February the British, in a final attempt to solve the impasse, released
the Monaghan prisoners from Derry Gaol whilst the IRA responded by allowing
twenty-six of the captured loyalists to go free. After careful diplomacy all prisoners
captured since January were released and the evacuation of British troops from
the Curragh resumed on 27 February. The feared confrontation had been
averted. However the real victims of the Clones affray were the people of Belfast,

particularly Catholics. Between the 6 and 25 February forty-three people were killed there (twenty-seven Catholics and sixteen Protestants). Thirty-one of these deaths occurred between 13 and 15 February. The deaths included the horrific bombing in Weaver Street where, on 13 February, a bomb was thrown into a Catholic schoolyard in the York Road area of the city. Two children were killed instantly, four others died later from their wounds in hospital. Father John Hassan called it 'a more horrible outrage than any that had hitherto disgraced this savage city'. Churchill agreed, saying in the Commons that 'It is the worst thing that has happened in Ireland in the last three years'.

Other horrors were to follow the next day. A nineteen-year-old Catholic man, James Rice, was attacked by a mob at 9 pm in Ravenscroft Street. His hands were tied behind his back and he was shot several times whilst on the ground. His attackers then battered his skull in with revolver butts for good measure. His mangled body was found dumped in an alley a few hours later. Bishop MacRory later blamed the Belfast violence on 'the doctrine of vicarious punishment according to which the Catholics of Belfast are made to suffer for the sins of their brethren elsewhere'. Throughout 1922 this pattern of border violence provoking costly sectarian clashes in Belfast was to be repeated many times. These events were further fuelled by the emotive funerals of the four Specials killed at Clones, all of which took place on 14 February in various parts of the North. On 21 February the IRA added another victim to the rapidly growing list when they shot dead another Special, twenty-one-year-old Hector Stewart, in Edlingham Street, Belfast. The Clones affray's list of victims had reached almost forty within only three days of the incident.

With the onset of even more gruesome violence in Belfast during March, including the horrific MacMahon murders, the Clones affray began to appear as only a minor border skirmish of little lasting consequence. During March 53 more people were to be killed in the North. The Clones affray became just one of countless brutal incidents whose seemingly relentless increase paved the way for one final attempt to resolve the Northern issue in the shape of the second Craig-Collins pact.

Despite its evident importance at the time, the Clones affray has been almost forgotten. This is bound up with the broader attitudes to the establishment of Northern Ireland. The ambiguities and brutality of the conflict in the North resulted in almost a conspiracy of silence, both sides having a vested interest in leaving such events where they lay. This has remained the case even despite the fact that almost 500 people lost their lives in Belfast alone during the 1920-2 period, the highest per capita total in Ireland during the whole revolutionary period. Critiques of the establishment of the Northern Ireland state inevitably focus on unionists' use of oppressive security measures and involvement in brutal acts of repression and murder. For Southern nationalists the Northern situation is a sorry tale of miscalculation, culminating in the shambolic Boundary Commission of 1925 and the virtual abandonment of the Northern

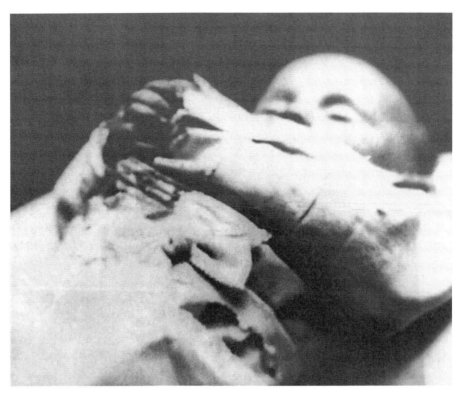

68. An infant victim of the Belfast violence c. 1922. Bishop MacRory laid
the blame on 'the doctrine of vicarious punishment according to which
the Catholics of Belfast are made to suffer for the sins of their brethren
elsewhere'. (George Morrison)

Catholic minority. They have preferred to hide behind a mantra of rhetoric on
their desire for Irish unity, whilst doing little constructively to bring it about. In
this sense both sides find the period fits uneasily into their respective national
stories. Unionists during this period fit more readily the role of besiegers of
the Catholic minority rather than the besieged of old, whilst nationalists prefer
to concentrate on the less morally ambiguous victory they obtained over the
British in the War of Independence rather than the squalid failure in the North.

The Clones affray also illustrates the shadowy and confused role of Michael
Collins, who, stuck in his cocoon of conspiracy, continued in his deluded belief
that an aggressive IRA policy could achieve similar results to those of the War of
Independence. His failure to understand the Northern situation meant that his policy
was at best a failure and at worst counter-productive, doing little else but confirming
unionist prejudices and highlighting the Northern Catholic minority's vulnerability.
The Clones affray signaled neither the end nor the beginning of a new phase in
North–South relations: it was a tragic accident that never should have happened.

Chapter 17

'A scrapping of every principle of individual liberty': the postal strike of 1922

Alexis Guilbride

> The unemployment is acute. Starvation is facing thousands of people. The official Labour Movement has deserted the people for the fleshpots of the empire. The Free State Government's attitude towards striking postal workers makes clear what its attitude towards workers generally will be.

Thus wrote Liam Mellows, IRA director of purchases, from his prison cell in Mountjoy Jail in September 1922, several weeks before his execution by the provisional government of Saorstat Éireann. The significance of this seminal incident, the first trades dispute faced by an Irish government, was not lost on Liam Mellowes or his contemporaries. Yet despite the fact that the strike, and the government's response to it, clearly exposed the inherent antagonisms between a nationalist bourgeoisie and an organised proletariat, it has gone virtually unrecorded in the history books, overshadowed by the national obsession with the details of the civil war which was still raging at the time.

The story of the postal workers' strike can be pieced together, however, from the records contained in the Postal and Telecommunications Workers Union archive, held in the Irish Labour History Museum. An examination of the twenty-two union files concerning the strike and its aftermath reveals a narrative of high drama that centred around the issue of the right to strike.

The strike was provoked by the provisional government's attempt to cut the 'cost of living' bonus, which was paid on a twice-yearly basis to all civil servants, including postal workers. Throughout the Great War civil servants in Britain and Ireland had been granted an allowance to shore up their wages against the dramatic inflation of the war years. After the war these allowances were retained as 'cost of living' bonuses to off-set against continuing rising prices. The government took the inflammatory step of introducing a cut in the bonus as early as March 1922, with the threat of further cuts to come. An emergency resolution issued in response by the Irish Postal Union pointed out that:

> Whereas the majority of the Irish Civil Service recently gained substantial additions to their permanent remuneration, the wages of the Post Office

staff are on practically the same level as those of thirty years ago. Any further reduction will bring Post Office wages to starvation level.

The union resolved to take 'the necessary steps for an immediate withdrawal of labour in the event of a reduction being enforced'.

Consequently the government agreed to the setting up of an independent commission of inquiry into wages and working conditions within the postal service, chaired by J.G. Douglas. Its interim report in May 1922 concluded that the cuts could not be borne by postal staff in the lower grades without serious hardship. It recommended instead that certain levels of wages in the postal service be immediately increased, and that any further cuts should be postponed until an Irish cost-of-living index was agreed upon, or until the commission produced its final report. The government, however, ignored the findings and drew up a cost-of-living index based on what the unions alleged were false figures. On the basis of these controversial figures further cuts were announced, to be put into effect in September 1922. 'In other and plainer terms', as an article in *Voice of Labour*, official organ of the Irish Transport and General Workers' Union, pointed out, 'a man who, in the opinion of the commissioners, could not reasonably bear a reduction of ten shillings in May, is deprived of fifteen shillings in September'.

The three unions representing postal workers, the Irish Postal Union, the Irish Postal Workers' Union and the Irish Post Office Engineering Union, were

69. September 1922—striking postal workers pose for the camera. (Irish Labour History Museum)

left with no option but to call for a strike. In anticipation of such action the Postmaster General, James J. Walsh, issued a 'special notice to the staff' on 6 September 1922, stating:

> In view of threats which have been made by sections of the staff to withdraw their labour because of the application of the Irish cost-of-living figure to the civil service bonuses, all civil servants should note that:
>
> 1) An officer withdrawing his labour automatically forfeits his position, and
> 2) In the event of subsequent reinstatement on settlement, reinstatement would not carry with it restoration of pension rights for the previous service or of continuous service.
>
> by command of the Postmaster General

The three postal unions came together on a temporary basis to form the United Postal Union, which promptly wrote to Thomas Johnson, secretary of the Irish Labour Party and Trade Union Congress, pointing out the intimidatory nature of the special notice. This letter (7 September 1922) refers to

> the bullying of his workers by a member of the government into dropping legitimate trade union methods of redressing their grievances. There is, indeed, an attempt to deny the right of government workers to be members of trade unions.

This was, in fact, precisely the stand taken by the government. The *Voice of Labour* commented:

> The government was appointed last Saturday afternoon. At the time previously appointed, namely, 6pm on Saturday, the strike began...The first act of the government was to issue on Saturday night the following proclamation:
>
>> The government does not recognise the right of civil servants to strike. In the event of a cessation of work by any section of the postal service, picketing, such as is permitted in connection with industrial strikes, will not be allowed.
>
> The workers in general, and Trade Unionists in particular, will not be silent. The right to strike is in danger and it must be defended.

When the women and men of the postal service withdrew their labour on 10 September, the police and military were ordered to take whatever action they deemed necessary to remove pickets from the streets. Initially the police carried out this onerous task with restraint, and at least one officer was dismissed for

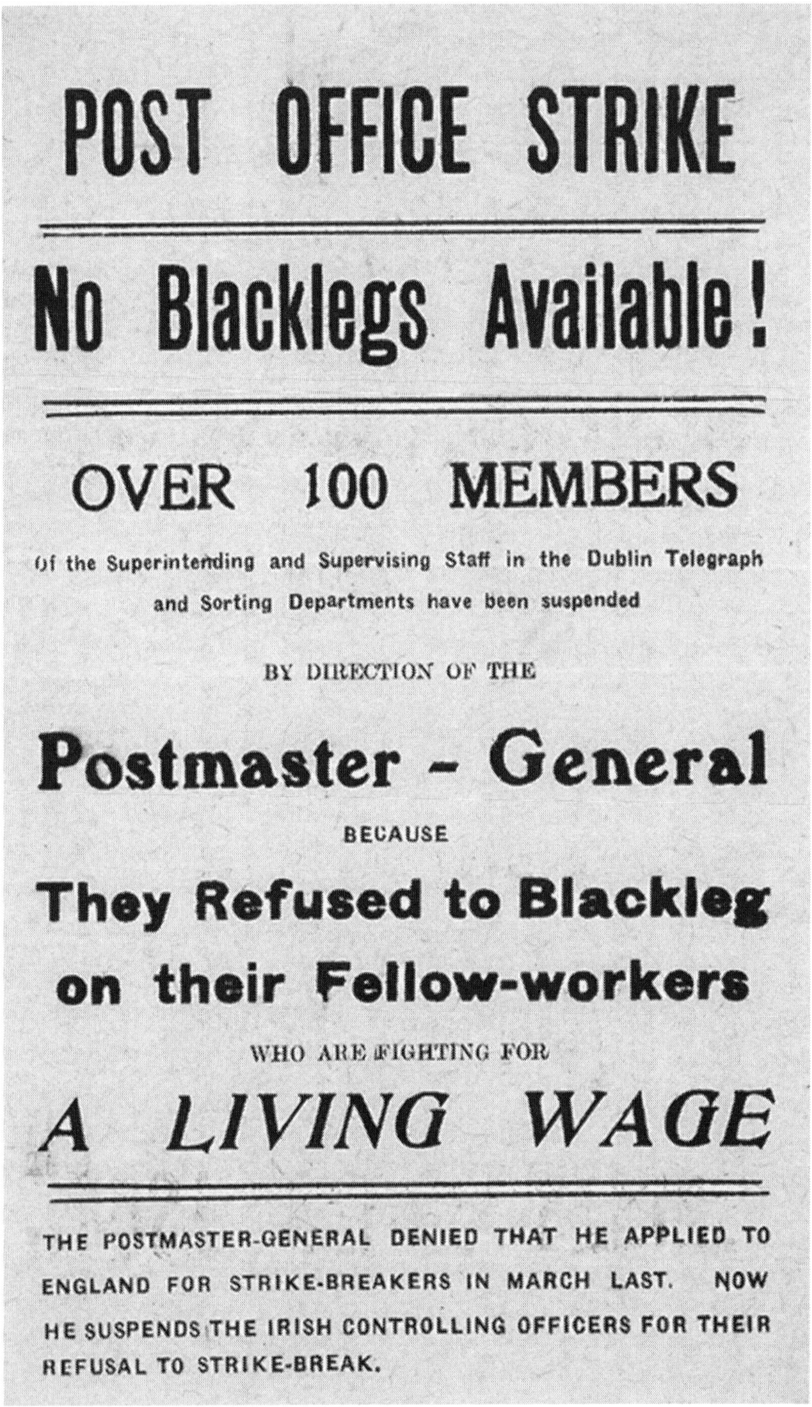

70. A poster issued in support of the strike.

refusing to arrest peaceful pickets on the grounds that he was unaware of any law they were breaking. (Despite appealing his dismissal, the officer was never reinstated.) As the strike continued and the military were called in, however, more brutal tactics were employed against the strikers.

The government's refusal on the Saturday to recognise the postal workers' right to strike was followed by a Dáil debate on Monday 11 September. The majority of the supporters of the government voted against the right of government employees to strike, as did the farmers' representatives. The Labour Party deputies and some independents voted in favour of the right to strike, but they were in a minority. The *Voice of Labour* listed the deputies who voted for and against by name and declared:

> The government has raised the issue above an ordinary wages dispute—it has raised it to the higher level of the right to strike and the right to picket. It is an issue and a challenge which the trade union movement cannot afford to ignore.

Members of the Free State army dressed in civilian clothes were already acting as strike-breakers, sorting post and delivering letters, and military escorts were being provided around the country for civilian blacklegs. An undated statement issued by the joint strike executive claimed that:

> Teachers and managers of certain city schools have been asked to supply lists of applicants for Post Office employment—in other words for blacklegging. Will they do so, or will the parents consent to have their children branded by the Free State government with the stigma of juvenile slaves? We shall see. We have the most reliable information that one or two notorious ex-members of the Black and Tans are at present in the service of the PMG [Postmaster General] in Dublin. In more than one instance ex-officials of the Post Office dismissed and imprisoned for theft of correspondence have been re-employed since the strike, and have now access to all kinds of public property in the Post Office.
>
> Early yesterday morning an armoured car (no. L13) made frequent and deliberate attempts to run down the pickets at the front and rere of the Rink sorting office.

This kind of statement from the joint strike executive was the forerunner to a strike bulletin which the unions began to issue on a daily basis in response to unfavourable press coverage. That a form of press censorship was in operation became clear when an advertisement favourable to the strike which was tendered by the Irish Women Workers' Union was refused by the *Evening Herald*, although it was eventually published by the *Daily Telegraph*. The strike bulletin typically contained accounts, for instance, of how unemployed men around the country were being warned that they would lose their unemployment benefit if they refused to take up scab work in the Post Office. A letter published in the bulletin from a political prisoner in Mountjoy stated that the governor had offered release to any men who were prepared to blackleg.

Issues arising from the strike continued to provoke heated debates in the Dáil. On Wednesday 13 September 1922 Labour deputies Thomas Johnson and Cathal O'Shannon both expressed their concern over the infringements of civil liberties resulting from the government's handling of the situation:

> We are here raising the question that we are raising, because of its effect on the general labour movement, and because of its effect upon the carpenter, the docker, the shop assistant, and every other worker at any other time. You are laying it down that military can disperse a picket, that military can fire at a picket or over the heads of a picket; that military can use terroristic methods to destroy a body of workers carrying on what I contend to be a legal operation...Is that the state of affairs to which we in Ireland have come at this day, that this government and this parliament find that the very first act of its ministry is an act of such a nature that all these things flow from it, that there is a scrapping of every principle of individual liberty?

The postal strike was rapidly becoming central to the whole question of where the Irish Revolution was going. The struggle for national independence had been, apparently inextricably, bound up with the struggle for social revolution, as embodied in the figure of James Connolly. The overthrow of the ruling classes by the Bolsheviks in Russia had impacted hugely on the ideology of the Republican movement while the battle against the foreign oppressor continued. In the aftermath of the achievement of the nationalist goal, however, the rift between those who supported the Treaty and those who were still holding out for the establishment of an independent republic was not the only division to manifest itself; those who had believed that they were fighting for a new order based on socialist principles were now compelled to face the bitter truth that the revolution had betrayed them. An article published in *The Voice of Labour* during the strike stated this new perception clearly when it concluded:

> The peaceful evolution of the Free State will mean the triumph of the landlord, large land-holding and big commercial classes. The orthodox politicians who have become the custodians of the republican principle have moved far from the policy of Connolly; they are neither qualified nor disposed to cut adrift from the environment or convention of graft and profit in which they were conceived and into which they were born as a party.

On 17 September 1922 one of the most dramatic incidents of the strike occurred when Miss Olive Flood was shot at close range and wounded by a Free State soldier while she was on picket duty in Merchant's Arch, Dublin. The reporting of this event in the *Irish Independent* was rejected by the strike executive who issued a statement:

> Today's newspaper account of the wounding of Miss Flood, telephone operator, is clearly that supplied by the military. The union's account of the incident was almost entirely suppressed.

The newspaper report claimed that, while shots had been fired into the air, Miss Flood's injury had been caused by a small piece of falling masonry dislodged by a bullet. The union's version of the incident was very different. According to statements from those who had been present at the scene, the soldier had ordered the pickets out of the Arch at gunpoint. As they began to move away he fired, and shot Miss Flood in the back. She was rushed to Jervis Street Hospital where it was discovered that the bullet had been deflected by a suspender buckle, so that she sustained only a flesh wound. Discretion would, no doubt, have contributed to preventing a more detailed discussion of the shooting of Miss Flood in the newspapers, given the delicate nature of her injury. Nonetheless, the shooting of a woman picket by Free State troops in the course of an official trades dispute caused outrage amongst the public in general, and increased support for the strikers.

A range of methods of undermining the strike were pursued at the instigation of the Postmaster General, James J. Walsh. Walsh, a former postal worker himself, had been an active member of Sinn Féin for several years, and had been one of the men responsible for the arrangements for the inauguration of Dáil Éireann. He had a reputation for radicalism, and early in 1919, as a method of provoking unrest amongst British soldiers stationed in Ireland, he had urged Sinn Féin to 'disseminate Bolsheviki literature to the military in this country'. As a minister in the new government, however, he was determined that nothing should interfere with the establishment of a successful independent Irish State, and used his power ruthlessly to crush the postal workers and make an example of them. An article in the strike bulletin commented:

> Mr. J.J. Walsh was once a prominent trade unionist. He waved the Red Flag in Liberty Hall some years ago. Strikes he then regarded as a meek and mild weapon. Nothing less than revolution would satisfy him. He is now a cabinet minister with £1,700 a year [Postal workers at this time were earning, on average, approximately £200 a year].

71. 'The Central Telegraph Office, Amiens street being closed in consequence of
the officials' strike. A large picket stationed here was placed under arrest after
having been warned to disperse'. (*Freeman's Journal*, 12 September 1922)

Later in the twenties, when Walsh had become director of elections for Cumann na
nGaedheal, a journalist who arrived to interview him in his office was confronted
with the spectacle of Walsh distributing brass knuckle-dusters to election workers.

An incident that was typical of Walsh's methods occurred in Limerick on 28
September 1922, the penultimate day of the strike. A Free State army officer
dressed as a woman, in skirt and shawl, attempted to pass the picket at the
Enquiry Office. When addressed by a striker the officer, armed with a knuckle-
duster, punched the man in the face. This was the signal for a general attack on
the picket by about twenty soldiers. Revolvers were produced but no shots were
fired. Instead the pickets were pistol-whipped. Fifteen strikers were seriously
injured in this attack, five of whom were women.

The striking clerks, postmen, sorters, telephonists, messengers, cleaners,
patrolmen and engineers suffered considerable financial hardship while the
dispute continued. Two cuts in the cost of living bonus meant that workers'
salaries had been dramatically reduced, while prices continued to rise. Now,
with no wages at all and a limited strike fund, the postal unions turned to
Congress and the Labour Party for assistance. They were advised to approach
other unions on an individual basis.

Ironically, the efforts of other unions to help the strikers were often seriously hampered by the effects of the strike. The Railway Clerks Association of Great Britain and Ireland sent their contribution to the strike fund in late October, apologising for the delay and explaining that the appeal for financial assistance issued by the joint postal unions had not reached their head office in London until the last day of the strike, due to the dislocation of the strike itself.

Alongside hardship and hunger, the postal workers had to contend with constant accusations of betraying the cause of national independence. A statement issued by the executive pointed out that

> The members of the government thought it was patriotic for the Post Office staff to go on strike on behalf of the Mountjoy hunger strikers and on the occasion of the Mountjoy executions, while the Chamber of Commerce then called us unpatriotic. Now, when we withdraw our labour for ourselves and our families, both parties call us unpatriotic.

The strike as a political weapon against a colonial administration had had the full support of the Sinn Féin party prior to independence; now that Sinn Féin was in power the use of the strike as a means for workers to protect their standards of living was perceived by the government as an unacceptable threat to the stability of the state. It was becoming increasingly obvious to the labour movement in Ireland that a native government based on privilege was at least as inimical to the interests of the working people as a foreign one had ever been. A leading article published in the *Voice of Labour* on 23 September 1922 remarked 'a foreign flag generally, perhaps invariably, denotes slavery, but national independence and a national flag do not inevitably or invariably denote human freedom'.

Eventually the strike came to an end on 29 September 1922, with a commitment from the government that the Douglas commission would proceed with further investigations into pay and conditions for postal workers. The United Postal Union issued a resolution on 2 October:

> That with a view to presenting a common front to the Department at the final sittings of the Commission, and for the purpose of facilitating the issue of the final report before December 1st, the executives of the Irish Postal Union, the Irish Postal Workers' Union and the Irish Post Office Engineering Union, agree to provisional amalgamation; the question of permanent amalgamation to be discussed by special conferences of each union, as early as possible after the final report of the commission.

In fact the IPU and the IPWU agreed to permanent amalgamation in 1923, when they became the Post Office Workers Union, but the IPOEU remained

72. Striking postal workers protest at harassment of pickets. (Irish Labour History Museum)

separate until 1989 when a merger resulted in the establishment of the Communication Workers' Union.

In a meeting with members of the Labour Party on 25 September 1922, President Cosgrave had given assurances that no victimisation of strikers would take place on settlement of the dispute. As soon as the strike was declared over, however, J. J. Walsh, the Postmaster General, dismissed the meeting with President Cosgrave as 'informal', thus invalidating any exchanges which had occurred. Walsh then proceeded to implement the most vicious methods of victimisation available to him. Experienced workers who had supported the strike were withdrawn on the grounds of trumped-up charges of incompetence and replaced by untrained staff who had been drafted in as strike-breakers; these same individuals who had provided scab labour throughout the strike were given permanent appointments without having to undergo the requisite medical and educational examinations; those refugees from the pogroms in Belfast who had been offered appointments in Dublin if they took up duty in the Rink sorting office during the strike and had refused, were forced to return to Belfast.

The hardest blow, however, was the government's decision to regard the strike as a break in service affecting pension rights and incremental rates.

In a letter to J. J. Walsh dated 5 May 1924 William Norton, general secretary of the POWU, wrote:

In 1920 when my union struck as a protest against the treatment of the Mountjoy hunger-strikers, its action was applauded and approved by the then leaders of the Sinn Féin party, who in many cases are now members of the government. From the point of view of the British administration the strike of its employees at that period had a grave political significance, and was, no doubt, viewed seriously. The only punishment, however, which was inflicted on my members was the stoppage of pay for the two days' absence.

My Executive desires me to contrast this decision of the then much maligned British administration with the action of the present administration on the occasion of the strike of 1922 in deferring increments, and to express regret that a native administration should be guilty of such vindictiveness and such hostility to trade union action.

Despite the constant efforts of the union, however, it took ten years before the incremental rates were restored and two more years before the issue of pensions was resolved. The 1922 strike and its aftermath seemed to bear out the truth of James Connolly's vision of the consequences of a nationalist revolution divorced from socialist principles:

'Let us free Ireland' says the patriot who won't touch socialism. Let us all join together and cr-r-rush the br-r-rutal Saxon. Let us all join together, says he, all classes and creeds. And, say the town workers, after we have crushed the Saxon and freed Ireland, what will we do? Oh, then you can go back to your slums, same as before. Whoop it up for liberty!

After Ireland is free, says the patriot who won't touch Socialism, we will protect all classes, and if you won't pay your rent you will be evicted same as now. But the evicting party, under command of the sheriff, will wear green uniforms and the Harp without the Crown, and the warrant turning you out on the roadside will be stamped with the arms of the Irish Republic. Now, isn't that worth fighting for?

Chapter 18

'Will the show go on?': the IRA's Civil War campaign against Dublin's cinemas and theatres

Gavin Foster

few nights after St Patrick's Day 1923, two men arrived at the Bohemian Picture House in Phibsborough, a suburb on the north side of Dublin. The Irish Free State was still in the throes of civil war, but social life was returning to normal and business in theatres and picture houses was booming. The men would have easily been mistaken for ordinary patrons, but instead of purchasing tickets, one stood guard while the other approached the manager, introduced himself as a representative of the IRA and ordered the cinema closed. The way both men kept their right hands concealed in their trench-coat pockets effectively conveyed the threat of violence behind their message. Ten minutes later, two men (possibly the same duo) entered the nearby Blacquiere Cinema and forced the projectionist to put up a slide announcing the theatre's closure by the IRA. Fearing reprisals, both establishments hastily cut short the night's entertainment. After a constable on patrol was alerted, members of the Dublin Metropolitan Police, detectives from the criminal investigation department and Free State troops converged on the scene, only to find both businesses shuttered with no sign of the cinemas' employees or patrons, much less of the IRA.

The events of that evening were part of a broader anti-treaty campaign to enforce a moratorium on public amusements as a protest against Free State executions and mass internment of republicans. The ban encompassed myriad forms of public entertainment—sports, films, plays, dances, races and hunts—and was to be enforced across the country, at least as far as the IRA's deteriorating military position allowed. But as the centre of Free State power, with a vibrant social scene drawing thousands of patrons to the movies every week, Dublin and its cinema trade became the boycott's focus. The short-lived campaign ultimately did little to forestall the anti-treaty movement's defeat and the rapid consolidation of post-revolutionary normality under the Free State. It did, however, succeed briefly in preoccupying the police and military while also creating tensions between the government and Dublin's theatre and cinema owners, thereby exposing some of the contradictions in and limits to the new state's 'business as usual' policy during the Civil War.

Politics and violence impinged on and interacted with the country's social life throughout Ireland's revolutionary period. In the pre-revolutionary years, the GAA (the Gaelic League), the literary revival scene and advanced nationalist groups like Sinn Féin provided alternative recreational outlets alongside their cultural and political *raisons d'être*. With the coming of the Great War, the Defence of the Realm Act gave the British government wide powers to proscribe organisations and events, provisions that were increasingly used against cultural and social activities linked to separatist nationalism. From mid-1920 the Restoration of Order in Ireland Act had extended the terms of the Defence of the Realm Act, while the escalating War of Independence increasingly disrupted everyday life, from commerce and transportation to the holding of popular recreations like dances, sports matches and hunts. Crown forces occasionally banned or disrupted social gatherings in the face of republican defiance, while in other instances the IRA interfered with recreational events, particularly hunts and other social activities associated with the Anglo-Irish gentry. With the 1921 truce everyday life began to return to normal, the popular appetite for sports and other amusements continuing unabated into the summer of 1922, when the burgeoning treaty split began to affect the public's access to entertainment.

The Provisional Government's opening assault on the IRA-held Four Courts on 28 June 1922 was followed by heavy fighting in northside Dublin's shopping, entertainment and business district. In the wake of the battle for Dublin, the *Freeman's Journal* described the fighting's impact on the entertainment landscape: the Metropole was turned into a Red Cross station and the La Scala Theatre became an artillery battery for Provisional Government troops, while the Corinthian, the Grand Central, the Pillar and other picture houses were 'situated right in the midst of military operations'. In a surreal twist, when the picture houses reopened by mid-July, patrons were entertained to newsreels of the fighting that had just raged on the streets outside. But while the cinema trade was not too adversely affected by the outbreak of war, 'business as usual' proved elusive. Taking advantage of the temporary closures caused by fighting, members of the cinema employers' association refused to reopen until employees consented to a twenty-five per cent wage cut first proposed in June. The ministry of labour succeeded in having the wage issue deferred until April 1923, but the wage dispute ultimately dragged on longer than the Civil War itself.

In the ensuing months, the heavy-handed methods employed by the National Army against stubborn pockets of IRA resistance, and the public's apparent acquiescence to Free State policies, contributed to the hardening of republican attitudes towards civilians that underlay the IRA's policy. Republicans were particularly aggrieved by the executions of captured volunteers, a development that few public bodies vigorously denounced once the precedent was established. In early March 1923, the news that groups of republican prisoners were taken out and blown up with mines at Ballyseedy, Killarney and Cahirciveen, County Kerry, provided the immediate catalyst for republicans' offensive against Irish social life.

The campaign against public amusements was announced on 14 March in a proclamation issued by Patrick (P. J.) Ruttledge, minister for home affairs in the underground 'Government of the Irish Republic'. Condemning Free State executions and mistreatment of internees, the proclamation obliquely referenced the 'tragedies of Kerry' when it accused the pro-treaty army of 'daily violations of the usages of war'. To bring attention to these 'crimes' and out of respect for the feelings of republican prisoners and their 'bereaved families', it concluded by ordering an indefinite period of 'national mourning' to be observed by the suspension of all sports and amusements.

Several of the recreations singled out—horse-racing, hunting and coursing—have deep roots in Irish rural life, but a specific reference to picture houses reflects the increasingly urbanised, electrified and consumerist nature of Irish society by the early twentieth century. In 1923 there were over 100 cinemas and theatres with projectors in the twenty-six counties (fifty-seven more could be found across the border). Dublin alone was home to about three dozen of these. Typical cinema fare consisted of Pathé Gazette newsreels (pre-screened by a Free State Army censor), Charlie Chaplin and Buster Keaton comedies, Sherlock Holmes productions and popular melodramas. As this was the era of the silent film, showings were accompanied by live piano, organ or even full orchestra. Beyond cinematic fare, Dubliners had a wide menu of performing arts to choose from, including pantomime, juggling, comedy, ventriloquists, dance and dramatic performances.

The day after the boycott was publicised, a majority of the city's cinemas and theatres failed to open. Instead, representatives of the theatre trade met with Minister for Home Affairs Kevin O'Higgins, who promised military protection and compensation for any damages if cinemas reopened. With the light heavyweight world championship between Senegalese boxer 'Battling Siki' (a.k.a. Ahmadou 'Louis' Mbarick Fall) and Clare-born American fighter Mike McTigue scheduled for St Patrick's Day at La Scala Theatre, O'Higgins also promised armed plainclothes guards for that event. A meeting of the Free State executive resulted in three further decisions: (1) the minister for defence would order the entertainment industry to continue 'business as usual' (including advertising), with fines for non-compliance; (2) republican prisoners would be punished with a suspension of 'privileges'; and (3) the press would not be permitted to report on the IRA's ban.

Sufficiently reassured, cinema/theatre proprietors agreed to resume business the following day, Friday 16 March. Nonetheless, the military circulated its order against future business closures, pointing out that acquiescence to such threats only served to encourage the IRA's 'conspiracy to obstruct the working of the government' and henceforth would be a punishable offence. Meanwhile, having received an IRA message threatening 'serious consequences' if Saturday's prizefight went ahead, La Scala's owners and both boxers were given police protection.

It is often assumed that the historic fight went ahead without incident, but in fact the IRA did attempt to disrupt it, albeit with negligible results. That night a powerful mine exploded behind the Pillar Picture House, throwing orchestra members from their seats and causing a stampede in Sackville Street. While the Pillar was assumed to have been the target, the *Freeman's Journal* surmised that the mine was intended to damage underground cables supplying power to La Scala and/or to down wires relaying the fight across the Channel. The bombing caused only minor damage, however, and the Pillar resumed its programme, while McTigue defeated 'Siki' after twenty rounds.

Its moratorium on amusements swiftly countered, the IRA escalated its threats against businesses. On 19 March, two men approached the Assembly Hall Picture House demanding to know why it had opened on St Patrick's Day. Although the owner was shaken, the DMP convinced her to stay open. Such was not the case at the Bohemian and Blacquiere that night, and both remained closed the following night despite promising the authorities otherwise. 21 and 22 March saw similarly mixed reactions: upon being served with a 'final warning' from the Dublin Brigade, two Camden Street proprietors stayed open with protection, but half a dozen other cinemas (including one on Talbot Street that was showing the Siki–McTigue fight) either did not open or closed hastily after receiving threats. Several of these ignored police orders to resume operations.

Over the next week the IRA began backing up its threats with actual violence. On 23 March the Carlton Picture House on Sackville Street had a hole blown in its entrance. Alerted to flames crawling along the fuse moments before the explosion, a military patrol rushed to the scene and exchanged gunfire with two fleeing 'Irregulars'. One of the perpetrators, described enigmatically as 'a man in a blue serge suit', escaped by shielding himself with a passerby, but his accomplice, identified as Volunteer Patrick O'Brien (twenty-six) of Clontarf, fell in a hail of bullets outside of the Masterpiece Picture House on Talbot Street. The only apparent fatality in the IRA's campaign against Dublin's picture houses, he reportedly uttered the cinematic dying words, 'I think I'm done for … Get me a priest.' On the 29 March the Fountain Picture House was targeted with a similar attack, only this time in broad daylight. According to witnesses, two women arrived at the James Street Chapel around 7.30 am and handed an attaché case to two waiting men. One of the latter was seen returning from the direction of the Fountain shortly before a petrol bomb exploded out front, causing minor damage. Other Dublin picture houses that were damaged in the IRA's anti-amusements campaign included the Grand Central Cinema, the Pillar and the Stella.

By early April the city's cinemas and theatres were functioning normally, and the IRA's campaign disintegrated into sporadic efforts to disrupt amusements elsewhere in the country. It is difficult, then, to dispute the press verdict that the IRA's moratorium proved a 'miserable failure'. Nevertheless, behind the scenes the IRA's actions did succeed in creating friction between local businesses and the government. Whereas the 'Theatre and Cinema Association (Ireland)' stressed the conditional nature of its cooperation with Free State orders to stay open and expectation of compensation for damages, following a dispute over extended closures during Holy Week Minister O'Higgins delivered a new ultimatum that any picture house that succumbed to IRA threats would be taken over and operated by the military. When one proprietor cited the 'simple business maxim' that owners should be 'at liberty to open when we think it would pay us, and to close when we think there will be a loss', O'Higgins's unsympathetic rebuttal illustrates how the government's authoritarian policy precluded rather than ensured 'business as usual'. 'Individual rights cannot always be regarded … in a vacuum,' O'Higgins argued, 'and when free exercise of individual rights clashes seriously with the general good it becomes a question of making a choice.' As such, theatre owners should accept 'any loss they have incurred as the result of Mr Rutledge's [*sic*] threatening letter as an investment to avert the utter extinction of their business'.

O'Higgins eventually relented on compensation claims. His initial response suggests, however, that anti-treatyites weren't the only impediment to the normalisation of conditions desired by many civilians. This is reinforced by the republican movement's attempt to revive its campaign against amusements in the summer/autumn of 1923 as a protest against continued internment months after the IRA dumped arms. This time the roles were reversed: with their agitation against renewed public safety measures, republicans were acting as the advocates of post-revolutionary normalisation, while the government's insistence on maintaining a war footing meant that 'business as usual' would elude the Free State for some time after the Civil War ended.

Chapter 19

The women who died for Ireland

Pádraig Óg Ó Ruairc

2018 marked several important milestones in the history of women's struggle in Ireland. The centenaries of the extension of the vote to women and the election of Constance Markievicz as the first female MP were widely celebrated. Less well known is that 2018 also marks the centenary of the death of Josephine McGowan, the first of several fatalities from Cumann na mBan, the republican women's organisation, during the Irish revolution. Although the central role that women played in the republican struggle from 1916 to 1923 is now widely known, the fact that a number of women died for that cause has been almost completely forgotten.

Following the enrolment of women in the Irish Citizen Army and the formation of Cumann na mBan as a female counterpart to the pre-war Irish Volunteers, female republicans were eager to carry arms and take the same risks as their male comrades. During the 1916 Rising, however, republican women were usually confined to cooking, first aid, messaging and signalling duties in support of male combatants. Although some women, such as Constance Markievicz and Margaret Skinnider, played a full role as combatants, they were the exceptions; no female combatants were killed during the 1916 Rising. (Nurse Margaretta Keogh, killed at the South Dublin Union, though frequently claimed as a member of Cumann na mBan, was in fact a civilian.)

Women undertook dangerous work transporting arms and explosives during the War of Independence but the only reference to their direct involvement in combat was in the IRA attack on Kilmallock RIC barracks in County Limerick, when one IRA Volunteer recalled that 'the Cumann na mBan women … used a rifle and boiled kettles as required'. Although generally barred from combat, republican women were still at risk of serious injury from their encounters with Crown forces, and at least two Cumann na mBan women were killed during that conflict.

Josephine 'Josie' McGowan was the first Cumann na mBan member killed during the Irish Revolution. She was from Dolphin's Barn, Dublin, and had served as a member of the Marrowbone Lane garrison during the 1916 Rising. On 22 September 1918 she attended a Cumann na mBan rally at Foster Place to protest against the internment of republican prisoners. The DMP baton-charged the assembly and during their onslaught a DMP constable struck McGowan several times on the head with his baton. Her comrades rescued her from the assault and took her to their medical outpost in Ticknock. She died there on 29 September 1918 and was buried in Glasnevin Cemetery. Decades later McGowan was posthumously awarded a War of Independence service medal, which included a 'Comhrac' bar—an award normally reserved for male combatants.

The second Cumann na mBan member killed was Margaret Keogh, a nineteen-year-old printer's assistant, who was fatally wounded by a gunshot in her home at Stella Gardens, Ringsend, Dublin, at 11.15 pm on 10 July 1921 during a series of raids by crown forces on the eve of the truce that ended the War of Independence. She died of her wounds two days later. If there was one woman who embodied all of the various strands entwined in the Irish Revolution it was Margaret Keogh. She was the captain of the Croke Ladies Hurling Club, a member of the Irish Clerical Workers Union, and an active member of Cumann na mBan. A year prior to her death, she had been arrested by Crown forces for refusing to give her name in English when questioned about her fund-raising activities for Conradh na Gaeilge (The Gaelic League), which was then a proscribed organisation. She was buried with military honours at Glasnevin Cemetery on 14 July 1921. Her grave is marked by a humble headstone bearing the inscription 'MARGARET KEOGH—DIED FOR IRELAND'.

During the truce a further two members of Cumann na mBan were killed. Margaret McAnaney was accidentally shot dead by an IRA Volunteer whilst delivering dispatches at Burnfoot, Co. Donegal, on 31 May 1922. The same day, Margaret McElduff died of an accidental gunshot wound whilst transporting a gun for the IRA in County Tyrone. In the Civil War, whether from political idealism or, more likely, military necessity, women were allowed to play a fuller military role. For example, Elizabeth Maguire acted as a quartermaster for the IRA's Dublin Brigade and was involved in twenty-eight attacks on Free State troops. Sighle Humphries led an armed Cumann na mBan unit in a raid on a hospital in October 1922 in an attempt to free a wounded IRA Volunteer guarded by Free State soldiers. The following month she was involved in a gun battle with the Free State Army when they captured Ernie O'Malley, the IRA's assistant chief-of-staff. It is unsurprising, therefore, that Cumann na mBan fatalities doubled during the Civil War.

The first Cumann na mBan member killed in that conflict was Mary Hartney from Limerick City. On 4 August 1922 the Free State Army used artillery to drive the IRA from the town of Adare, County Limerick. The Dunraven Arms Hotel, where the republicans had set up their military headquarters, suffered a direct hit during the opening barrage. A short time later a correspondent from the Free State Army's publicity department reported that 'all the rooms in the building were found to be bespattered with blood, showing that there must have been fairly severe casualties amongst the irregulars'. In fact only one member of the garrison had been killed—Mary Hartney. She had been working as part of a first aid unit when killed instantly by the shelling. She was buried in the republican plot of Mount St Lawrence Cemetery, Limerick, on 7 August 1922.

The next member of Cumann na mBan to be killed by the Free State Army was Lily Bennett from Aughrim Street, Dublin. The Republican Prisoners' Defence Committee held a public rally each Sunday in O'Connell Street. On 18 November 1922 Lily Bennett was attending the demonstration when Free State troops passing by in a motor convoy attacked the protesters with machine-gun fire from an armoured car. Charlotte Despard, who had been addressing the meeting, later insisted that the National Army had opened fire without provocation. Seven people were seriously wounded in the attack, including Lily Bennett, who was shot in the back and died a short time later.

Another member of Cumann na mBan, Margaret Dunne from Cappaleigh South near Castletown in west Cork, was shot dead by the Free State Army six months later. On 8 April 1923 a Free State soldier was wounded during a gunfight with two IRA volunteers at Adrigole. Approximately ten minutes later the Free State troops spotted Dunne conversing with a third IRA Volunteer who had not been involved in the attack. In an apparent act of reprisal for the wounding of his comrade, Captain Hassett of the Free State Army drew a gun and opened fire on the pair, shooting Margaret Dunne dead. Throughout the Civil War Cumann na mBan had rendered military honours at the funerals of IRA volunteers killed in action, but for Dunne's funeral the situation was reversed, as the men of the IRA came out of hiding and risked capture and execution to pay tribute to their fallen female comrade.

The final member of Cumann na mBan to die as a result of the conflict appears to have been Annie 'Nan' Hogan from Cratloe, County Clare. Hogan had organised safe houses during the War of Independence and was leader of the East Clare Brigade of Cumann na mBan. Late in 1922 the republican prisoners in Limerick jail had attempted to escape by digging a tunnel. The plot was betrayed, however, and on the night of the escape attempt Free State soldiers arrested seven Cumann na mBan women outside the prison, including Nan Hogan. She was interned without trial in Kilmainham Jail and went on hunger strike in March 1923 for better conditions and prisoner-of-war status. The hunger strike was eventually called off when it became obvious that the Free State authorities would not concede their demands. Unfortunately, this was too late to save Annie Hogan. She was released in September 1923 and died a short time later. Her family and friends attributed the twenty-four-year-old's premature death to her hunger strike and the conditions she had suffered in prison.

Surprisingly, the sacrifice of these Cumann na mBan women who died for their cause has been forgotten not only by the Republican movement but also by historians and academics. Apart from notable works such as Sinéad McCoole's

No Ordinary Women (2003), which mentions the deaths of Hogan and Dunne, and Mary McAuliffe and Liz Gillis's *We Were There—77 Women of the Easter Rising* (2016), which details the death of McGowan, almost all histories of Cumann na mBan ignore the sacrifice of these women.

Today the men of the IRA who fell in the struggle for Irish freedom are honoured by hundreds of monuments nationwide. The boys of Na Fianna Éireann, the republican youth organisation, are commemorated by a monument dedicated specifically to them in St Stephen's Green in Dublin. But what of the women? There are currently at least four statues of Constance Markievicz (one in County Sligo and three others in Dublin City). There is also an information plaque in Wynn's Hotel, Dublin, marking it as the place where the inaugural meeting of Cumann na mBan was held in 1914. Nevertheless, in the context of Ireland's 'Decade of Centenaries', which inevitably includes the centenaries of the deaths of Josephine McGowan and her comrades in Cumann na mBan, the question now arises as to why no national memorial has ever been erected commemorating all of the women of Cumann na mBan and the girls of the Clan na nGaedheal Girl Scouts who sacrificed so much for the same cause during the 1916 Rising, the War of Independence, and the Civil War.

Select Bibliography

Abbott, Richard, *Police Casualties in Ireland, 1919–1922* (Dublin, 2000).

aan de Wiel, Jerome, *The Irish Factor, 1899–1919: Ireland's Strategic and Diplomatic Importance for Foreign Powers* (Dublin, 2008).

Borgonovo, John, *Spies, Informers and the Anti-Sinn Féin Society* (Dublin, 2006).

Crowley, John, Donal Ó Drisceoil and Mike Murphy (eds), John Borgonovo (associate ed.), *Atlas of the Irish Revolution* (Cork, 2017).

Foley, Michael, *The Bloodied Field: Croke Park, 21 November 1920* (Dublin, 2015).

Garvin, Tom *1922: The Birth of Irish Democracy* (Dublin, 1996).

Hart, Peter (ed.), *British Intelligence in Ireland: The Final Reports* (Cork, 2002).

Hart, Peter, *The IRA at War, 1916-23* (Oxford, 2003).

Hopkinson, Michael, *Green Against Green: The Irish Civil War* (Dublin, 1988).

Hopkinson, Michael, *The Irish War of Independence* (Dublin, 2002).

Kissane, Bill, *The Politics of the Irish Civil War* (Oxford, 2005).

Kotsonouris, Mary, *Retreat from Revolution: The Dáil Courts, 1919-23* (Dublin 1994).

Lawlor, Pierse, *The Burnings, 1920* (Cork, 2009).

Lawlor, Pierse, *The Outrages, 1920–1922* (Cork, 2011).

Leeson, D.M., 'Select document: the Prescott-Decie letter', Irish Historical Studies, vol. 38, no. 151 (May 2013), 511-522.

O'Connor, Emmet, *Reds and the Green: Ireland, Russia and the Communist Internationals, 1919–43* (Dublin, 2004).

Ó Ruairc, Padraig Óg, *Revolution: A Photographic History of Revolutionary Ireland, 1913–23* (Cork, 2011)

Ó Ruairc, Padraig Óg, *Truce: Murder, Myth and the Last Days of the Irish War of Independence* (Cork, 2016).

Poland, Pat, *For Whom the Bells Tolled: A History of Cork Fire Services* (Cork, 2010).

Phoenix, Eamon, *Northern Nationalism: Nationalist Politics, Partition and the Catholic Minority in Northern Ireland, 1890-1940* (Belfast, 1994).

Silvestri, Michael, *Ireland and India: Nationalism, Empire and Memory* (Basingstoke, 2009).

Reynolds, John, *The Templemore Miracles: Jimmy Walsh, Ceasefires, and Moving Statues* (Stroud, 2019).

Townshend, Charles, *The Republic: The Fight for Irish Independence, 1918-23* (London, 2012).

Yeates, Padraig, *A City in Turmoil: Dublin, 1919–21* (Dublin, 2013).

Yeates, Padraig, *A City in Civil War: Dublin, 1921–23* (Dublin, 2015).

Walsh, Maurice, *Bitter Freedom: Ireland in a Revolutionary World* (London, 2015).